Harry Potter™

The CHARACTER *Vault*

by Jody Revenson

Titan
BOOKS

An Insight Editions Book

Contents

CHAPTER 3: STUDENT ROBES & QUIDDITCH SPORTSWEAR

CHAPTER 4: THE TRIWIZARD TOURNAMENT

CHAPTER 5: CELEBRATIONS

CHAPTER 6: THE ORDER OF THE PHOENIX

CHAPTER 7: DARK FORCES

CHAPTER 8: MINISTRY OF MAGIC

CHAPTER 9: FAMILIES

Introduction

To the readers of author J.K. Rowling's Harry Potter book series, the story's characters are as familiar to them as their families, friends, and neighbors. They know what Harry Potter's lightning-bolt scar looks like, as well as Hermione Granger's Yule Ball dress and every initialed sweater that Ron Weasley received from his mother at Christmas. They know that once they pass through the Leaky Cauldron, with its seemingly eccentrically dressed patrons, they will find themselves in a world populated by an ancient and amazing magical society that exists clandestinely alongside their Muggle one. So the bar for the film versions of the books was set about as high as it could go. Producer David Heyman, production designer Stuart Craig, and director of the first two films, Chris Columbus, were tasked with bringing Rowling's work to the screen. "I thought it was incredibly important to be as faithful as possible . . . bringing to life their world as it was written," says Columbus. To that end, the filmmakers brought together the magic-worthy skills of highly accomplished costume designers, hair and makeup artists, concept artists, special effects designers, and craftspeople of a wide variety of disciplines, and the outstanding talents of the finest British actors and actresses to realize the characters for the Harry Potter films.

Past movies had habitually portrayed magical folk based on well-known stereotypes. Chief makeup artist Amanda Knight, who worked on all eight Harry Potter films, explains, "We knew we wanted to get away from the idea that all witches and wizards have long hooked noses and warts. I think that look is rather cheesy. You can't have everyone going around looking incredibly 'witchy' and weird. You've got to remember that all these witches and wizards have to get by in a contemporary Muggle world."

Though the wizarding world is distinctive from its Muggle counterpart, it still needed to be recognizable. So, in addition to needles, pins, and sewing machines, Judianna Makovsky, costume designer for *Harry Potter and the Sorcerer's Stone*, used research as an important tool. "Although," she says, "it's actually very difficult to design something where there are no boundaries. All research is open to you, and that's when things can get confusing. You can draw inspiration from anywhere, from ancient Greece to *Vogue* magazine. So part of the art of designing is to weed things down." Makovsky feels that one of her starting points was a discussion she had with Chris Columbus about the illustrations in author Charles Dickens's books. "When you

TOP: *One possible wizard's hat, sketched for* Harry Potter and the Sorcerer's Stone *by Ravi Bansal;* ABOVE: *Sixth-year students respond to a Potions class challenge in* Harry Potter and the Half-Blood Prince—*(left to right) Padma Patil (Afshan Azad), Dean Thomas (Alfred Enoch), Hermione Granger (Emma Watson), Neville Longbottom (Matthew Lewis), Ron Weasley (Rupert Grint), Lavender Brown (Jessie Cave), Leanne (Isabella Laughland), Seamus Finnigan (Devon Murray);* OPPOSITE: *Visual development artwork by Adam Brockbank of Hermione meeting Hagrid's giant half-brother, Grawp, in* Harry Potter and the Order of the Phoenix.

look at the original character drawings," she explains, "they have crooked suits, slightly smashed top hats, nothing is exact. They're elegant, but there's something a little disturbed about them. I think we all liked that vision."

Makovsky also needed to create the clothing worn by the students and teachers of the film's main location, a thousand-year-old educational institution, Hogwarts School of Witchcraft and Wizardry. "I always called it 'scholastic wizardry,'" she says. "We had already honed in on certain time periods we liked, and so felt that one natural parallel would be English boarding schools of the nineteenth-century." Makovsky blended in academic robes from the Renaissance as well as ideas from the Edwardian, Elizabethan, and medieval eras. The designer met with J.K. Rowling several times, "and we didn't discuss clothing. We talked about the characters and who they were; we talked about color and atmosphere. I only had to show her a fabric or a shape, and she'd say instantly if it was right or wrong."

Lindy Hemming was the costume designer for the second film, *Harry Potter and the Chamber of Secrets*. Hemming consulted with Chris Columbus as well, about the already established characters and the new characters to the story. "There was an overall look, especially inside Hogwarts," says Hemming, "and he wanted to keep the school uniforms and most of the principle characters as they were. Not meaning you had to keep them in the same costumes, of course, because new scenes dictated that they wear new clothes, but we needed to ensure that these followed the tone of the character's previous outfits." Hemming also had to deal with the massive amounts of extras on the set. "We had an army of people who exercised enormous discipline in checking everything out in the morning and checking everything back in at the end of the day." A printed reference was issued for each character, showing who they were and what they were supposed to wear—a specific hat and cloak combination, for example, or if they smoked a pipe or carried a broom—with even more details for

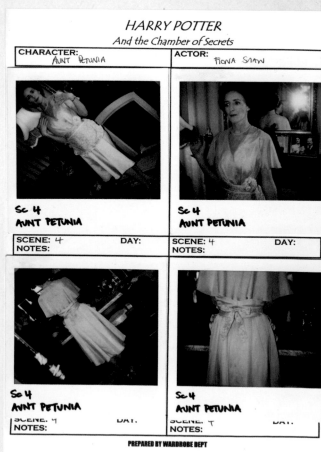

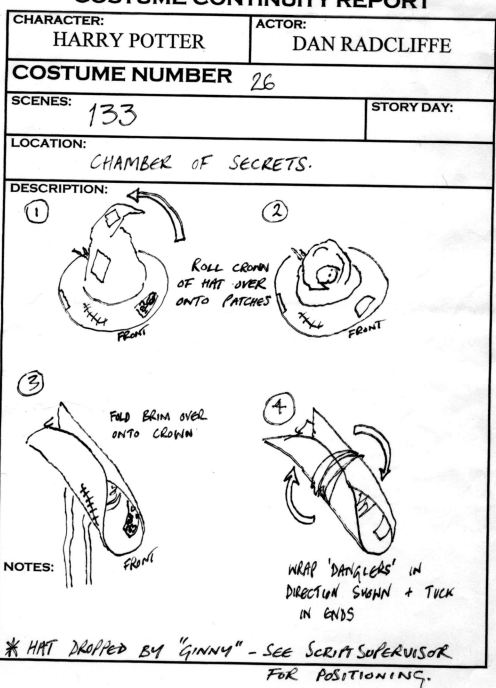

HARRY POTTER
The Chamber Of Secrets
COSTUME CONTINUITY REPORT

CHARACTER: Dumbledore

AC[...]

COSTUME NUMBER:

SCENES: 135

LOCATION: Int. Dumbledore's Offic[...]

DESCRIPTION:

Under-robe - Purple silk robe with length of front and gold/purple silk

Boots - Brown suede boots with gold

Hat - Red/Gold/purple patchwork a[...] shape with stencilled gold s[...]

Gown - heavy red/bronze silk sleeves in red/gold shot gauze w[...] Crown worn open.

Belt - Brown leather belt with large gold buckle. Crossed ca[...]

NOTES:

HARRY POTTER
Chamber of secrets
COSTUME CONTINUITY REPORT

CHARACTER:	ACTOR:
HARRY POTTER	DAN RADCLIFFE

COSTUME NUMBER 26

SCENES:	STORY DAY:
133	

LOCATION: CHAMBER OF SECRETS.

DESCRIPTION:

① ROLL CROWN OF HAT OVER ONTO PATCHES ②

③ FOLD BRIM OVER ONTO CROWN

④ WRAP 'DANGLERS' IN DIRECTION SHOWN + TUCK IN ENDS

NOTES:

✱ HAT DROPPED BY "GINNY" - SEE SCRIPT SUPERVISOR FOR POSITIONING.

OPPOSITE TOP: *Nadine Mann (center) and Sharon Nicholas (right) refresh makeup on Daniel Radcliffe for* Harry Potter and the Deathly Hallows – Part 2; *OPPOSITE BOTTOM: Continuity shots of Fiona Shaw as Petunia Dursley, taken for* Harry Potter and the Chamber of Secrets. *Continuity shots act as reference for the costume department; THIS PAGE: Costume continuity reports also provide information to the costume crew to ensure each outfit looks exactly the same in each shot. On the left, a list of what Dumbledore is wearing in a specific scene; on the right, instructions on the correct way to wrap the Sorting Hat when Fawkes carries it to Harry in the Chamber of Secrets.*

the main characters, including continuity shots to duplicate how they looked for each scene, which might include the placement of bandages for Harry's latest Quidditch injury or how to tie Professor Lockhart's cravat.

Director Alfonso Cuarón brought a new vision to *Harry Potter and the Prisoner of Azkaban*, and Jany Temime, who became costume designer for the remainder of the series, agreed with his approach. "I was really pleased that he thought, like me, as the stories were getting darker and the children were getting older, we should go for something harder." Instead of taking her inspiration from Dickens, as Temime explains, "I took my inspiration from the street. The wizarding world is a secret society, and they have their own traditions and their own culture, but they cannot ignore the modern world; they live parallel to it. They constantly have access to it. You don't have to dress up in historical clothing to have a wizard film. They don't all have to be in velvet. They can have pointed hats and long robes and their own couture, but they can also have blue jeans." Temime and Cuarón also agreed that as the children were now teenagers, they would feel the need to express their individuality, whether it be in school robes and more and more frequently, Muggle wear. One directive, however, was that no branding or logos appear on the Muggle clothes (although sharp-eyed viewers will occasionally see Converse™ sneakers).

Amanda Knight and hair stylists Eithne Fennell, who worked on *Harry Potter and the Sorcerer's Stone* through *Harry Potter and the Goblet of Fire*, and Lisa Tomblin, who continued through *Harry Potter and the Deathly Hallows – Part 2*, also embraced this policy. "The brief was always to make things as timeless as possible so that you

couldn't date anything," explains Knight. "We didn't want them to wear obvious makeup. We'd take care of any spots with concealer, but we tried to keep everything as natural as possible." Knight admits that she and her crew often needed to act as the "makeup police," monitoring young actresses who hid things in their pockets. "You'd always catch them in the girls' rooms putting on loads of mascara and lip gloss in case they saw Dan or Rupert."

Creating a costume from start to finish averages several months of work. In addition to reading the script and consulting the books, Temime considers the actor playing the role. Sketches are made, the director is consulted, and then samples are made for a fitting session. Hair and makeup are brought in, and "We try to establish that character with the actor or the actress," she says. "After that we make the costume, have another fitting and a show-and-tell, and change what has to be changed. After final alterations, we break it down, which means we age it or make it appear damaged. It's a very, very long process." In addition to making several versions for the actor, and often at different stages of wear, duplicates are made for their doubles and stunt doubles. More than twenty-five thousand items of clothing were created for the Harry Potter films, including six-hundred plus school uniforms—new robes had to be created each year for the growing children.

Characters are more than clothing, hair, and makeup, and so property master Barry Wilkinson, prop modeler Pierre Bohanna, draftsman Hattie Storey, and concept artists including Adam Brockbank provided wands, eyeglasses, and a Frog Choir conductor's batons. Death Eater masks and armor were envisioned by concept artist Rob Bliss and constructed by leather makers and metalworkers. Creature effects supervisor Nick Dudman and his crew crafted a magical eye, webbed feet and hands, and a large floating Muggle. Costumers also fashioned a Sorting Hat, an Invisibility Cloak, and myriad crocheted creations by Molly Weasley. And it goes without saying—no, of course it should be said—that the actors and actresses who inhabit these characters were vital to the mix.

Following is a corpus of costume sketches, visual development art, behind-the-scenes information, movie stills, and actor commentary that shows how these beloved characters came to life on-screen for the Harry Potter films.

SC·73
SORTING HAT
(TEACHERS P.O.V)

OPPOSITE TOP: *Sketches of Mundungus Fletcher for* Harry Potter and the Deathly Hallows – Part 1 *drawn by costume illustrator Mauricio Carneiro for costume designer Jany Temime;* OPPOSITE BOTTOM: *The first meeting of Dumbledore's Army in* Harry Potter and the Order of the Phoenix; TOP ROW: *Touchups on scars, costumes, and makeup—(left to right) Brendan Gleeson (Mad-Eye Moody) on the set of* Deathly Hallows – Part 1; *Beryl Anne Cohen puts final touchups on Voldemort's final costume for* Harry Potter and the Deathly Hallows – Part 2; *Emma Watson (in the Ministry of Magic set;* ABOVE: *Continuity shot of the Sorting Hat.*

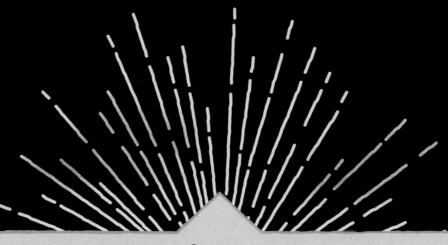

Chapter 1

HOGWARTS STUDENTS

HARRY POTTER

itting in is a perceptible theme throughout the world of Harry Potter, perhaps no more plainly showcased than in the hand-me-down clothes Harry himself wears in his first appearances on-screen in *Harry Potter and the Sorcerer's Stone*. Forced to live with his aunt and uncle, Harry is relegated to wearing his considerably larger cousin Dudley's castoffs, so overwhelming in size that he literally doesn't "fit in." Then Harry receives his letter from Hogwarts.

This, of course, needed to be reflected in his developing costume design. Judianna Makovsky, costume designer for *Harry Potter and the Sorcerer's Stone*, wanted to ensure that Harry's immersion into Diagon Alley and the wizarding world, coming from the middle-class Muggle environment of Privet Drive, evoked the same sense of amazement that viewers felt upon Dorothy's entrance into the Emerald City in *The Wizard of Oz*. "Harry is going on a journey to a world he is not part of it yet," says Makovsky. "I felt that for the first film you should feel Harry's awe at entering this whole new world that he could never imagine." For that purpose, Makovsky designed wizarding wear that suggested another time period recognizable to modern viewers, but still felt as if it could coexist with today's world. "But once Harry becomes part of Hogwarts," Makovsky continues, "he fits in with the world."

FIRST APPEARANCE:
Harry Potter and the Sorcerer's Stone

ADDITIONAL APPEARANCES:
Harry Potter and the Chamber of Secrets
Harry Potter and the Prisoner of Azkaban
Harry Potter and the Goblet of Fire
Harry Potter and the Order of the Phoenix
Harry Potter and the Half-Blood Prince
Harry Potter and the Deathly Hallows – Part 1
Harry Potter and the Deathly Hallows – Part 2

HOUSE:
Gryffindor

OCCUPATION:
Hogwarts Student, Gryffindor Seeker, Triwizard Tournament Champion, Chosen One

MEMBER OF:
Head of Dumbledore's Army

ADDITIONAL SKILL SET:
Parseltongue

PATRONUS:
Stag

PRECEDING PAGE: *Harry and Hermione wait for the right time to save Buckbeak in* Harry Potter and the Prisoner of Azkaban; *INSET:* Harry holds the Golden Snitch in Harry Potter and the Sorcerer's *Stone; ABOVE:* Harry is yet to "fit in" to costume designer Judianna Makovsky's Dickensian Diagon Alley *in* Sorcerer's Stone; *RIGHT: Sketch of Jany Temime's revised student robes for* Prisoner of Azkaban. *Costume illustration by Laurent Guinci; OPPOSITE: Publicity photo for* Harry Potter and the Deathly Hallows – Part 1.

Fans should note that the filmmakers made and tested out a version of Harry's outfit from the cover of the American *Harry Potter and the Sorcerer's Stone* novel. "Every country has a different illustration on the cover," says Makovsky, "but we made the one with the red-and-white rugby shirt, jeans, and Converse. Then we put him in the wizard gown and it just didn't work. Everybody wanted it, and every once in a while we'd put it on Harry, but Chris [Columbus] would say, no, it just doesn't work." Makovsky believes that the choice of uniformity for the wizarding school robes to establish the school's atmosphere worked better than the more casual outfit, "though it might have worked in the third movie."

When costume designer Jany Temime came aboard for *Harry Potter and the Prisoner of Azkaban*, director Alfonso Cuarón had already made the decision that the growing kids should begin wearing more contemporary clothes along with their school robes. This allowed Temime to develop individual color schemes to be a visual complement for each character. Temime thought of Harry Potter as "an outlaw. He's a kid who's not sure where he belongs. I thought, this is a lonely boy." The designer dressed him in very soft, muted colors: gray-blues, navies, and monochromatic checks. "You know when you feel you don't belong, when you don't feel good in your skin, you don't like to wear bright colors." One exception was the use of Gryffindor scarlet, which Harry would often wear during battle scenes with Voldemort or his Dark forces.

Several cosmetic adjustments were needed to bring the character from the page to the screen. In the books, Harry's eyes are green. Blue-eyed Daniel Radcliffe was fitted with contact lenses, but as happens in a small percentage of the population, his eyes reacted badly, becoming irritated and swollen. (This is evident in the last scene of *Harry Potter and the Sorcerer's Stone*, the only time Radcliffe appears on-screen with green, though red-infused, eyes.) The decision was quickly made to allow Harry's

TOP: *Harry Potter wears a hooded sweatshirt in* Harry Potter and the Prisoner of Azkaban. LEFT: *One of the thousands of pairs of Harry's glasses;* BELOW: *Interchangeable separates became the fashion for Hogwarts uniforms starting with* Prisoner of Azkaban. *Illustration by Laurent Guinci;* OPPOSITE TOP TO BOTTOM: *Continuity shots for* Harry Potter and the Sorcerer's Stone.

SC. 13 →
HARRY

SC. 12
HARRY

GAP FLAT FRONT SLIM FIT · 34×30
T SHIRT
SHIRT

Invisibility Cloak

Several versions of Harry Potter's Invisibility Cloak, given to him for Christmas by Albus Dumbledore in Harry Potter and the Sorcerer's Stone, were constructed by the costume department out of a thick velvet fabric that was dyed and then imprinted with astrological and Celtic symbols. There was a fully realized and lined cloak that Daniel Radcliffe (Harry Potter) would use to hold or to wear over a suit made of green-screen material. The version used to make him invisible was lined on its interior with green-screen material. Radcliffe would flip the cloak so that the green side would face up when he placed it over himself.

Ron and Harry learn about the Invisibility Cloak. In post-production, the green-screen material will be removed from inside of the cloak so on-screen Harry's body will appear invisible.

Harry Potter and Lord Voldemort duel in Little Hangleton graveyard in concept art by Adam Brockbank for Harry Potter and the Goblet of Fire.

Stinging Jinx

When Harry, Ron, and Hermione are captured by Snatchers in Harry Potter and the Deathly Hallows – Part 1, *Hermione performs a Stinging Jinx so that Harry won't be recognizable. Creature effects designer Nick Dudman created three progressive stages of makeups for the jinx, as the spell eventually wears off over the course of several scenes. In its most intense phase, Daniel Radcliffe had several prosthetics applied to his face, including one with a swollen fake eye. Dudman strove to ensure that even though the audience would know who it was, the disguise would be convincing enough to believe that Voldemort's emissaries wouldn't recognize Harry. Amanda Knight recalls that although it was difficult for the actors and crew to see Radcliffe so disfigured, it was more difficult for the actor—it took four hours to apply the makeup, and Radcliffe wasn't allowed to eat anything until the makeup was removed.*

TOP: *The result of Hermione's Stinging Jinx charm;* ABOVE: *Daniel Radcliffe, double Ryan Newbery (left), and stunt double Marc Mailley (right) in Stinging Jinx makeup.*

eyes to be blue in the film. Radcliffe was also equipped with the iconic glasses, made out of a nickel alloy. Shortly after filming began, the actor developed blemishes, not completely out of line for an adolescent, but Radcliffe's father, Alan, noticed that the spots occurred in a perfect circle around each eye that matched where the glasses sat on his son's face. It was discovered that Radcliffe had an allergy to nickel, and so the frames were swapped out for a safer material. The glasses rarely had lenses in them, in order to avoid reflections of the lights or cameras. After the final film, Radcliffe chose to take his first and last pair of glasses as a souvenir.

Harry's scar was stenciled daily onto his forehead via a fixed template, and then built up with prosthetic scar material. Chief makeup artist Amanda Knight, who worked on all eight Harry Potter films, recalls that in his younger years, "He used to pick off his scar when he was in class. We had a school on site, where the children would be taught, and he'd come back to the set with it hanging off." Knight adjusted Harry's makeup very subtly according to the circumstances of the scene. "When Voldemort was near Harry, we'd make him slightly paler," Knight explains. "At the same time, we'd make Harry's scar stronger, redder, and more angry looking when Voldemort was close. It shouldn't jump out at you from the screen, but I think in its way, it helped the actors and added to the feel of the scene." It's estimated that Harry Potter's scar was applied more than five thousand times: two thousand times on Daniel Radcliffe, and 3,800 times on his stunt doubles.

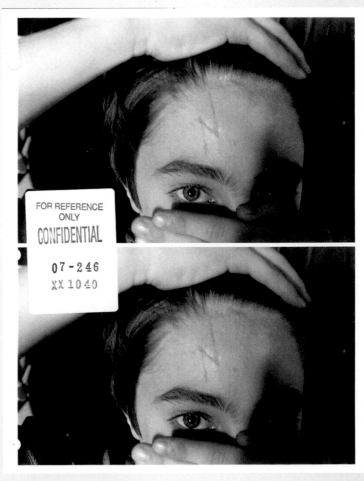

ABOVE: *Continuity shots of Daniel Radcliffe referencing one of the 2,000 or more iterations of Harry Potter's scar;* OPPOSITE TOP: *Harry encounters Dementors in* Harry Potter and the Order of the Phoenix.

HARRY'S WAND

J.K. Rowling's initial concept for the wizard's wands was that they were "just like an old stick," says draftsman Hattie Storey, so in the first two films, the wands were mostly simple, straight, and unembellished. For *Harry Potter and the Prisoner of Azkaban*, director Alfonso Cuarón wanted to reassess the look of the wands, making them more personal to the wizard, and had several types of unique wands made up for the cast to choose from. Daniel Radcliffe chose a wand with a decidedly organic look to it. Harry's wand was crafted from Indian rosewood, which the prop makers selected for its beautiful deep red color. The "bark" is a sculpted interpretation, but the hewing was done on a real piece of wood. "The top was cast from a tree burr," explains prop modeler Pierre Bohanna. "It's a naturally occurring piece of wood that grows at the bottom of the tree. This gives it a lot more character in, essentially, a very small piece of wood." Radcliffe went through almost seventy wands while filming the Harry Potter series.

"I'm just Harry.
Just Harry."

Harry Potter, *Harry Potter and the Sorcerer's Stone*

RON WEASLEY

FIRST APPEARANCE:
Harry Potter and the Sorcerer's Stone

ADDITIONAL APPEARANCES:
Harry Potter and the Chamber of Secrets
Harry Potter and the Prisoner of Azkaban
Harry Potter and the Goblet of Fire
Harry Potter and the Order of the Phoenix
Harry Potter and the Half-Blood Prince
Harry Potter and the Deathly Hallows – Part 1
Harry Potter and the Deathly Hallows – Part 2

HOUSE:
Gryffindor

OCCUPATION:
Hogwarts Student, Gryffindor Keeper (sixth year)

MEMBER OF:
Dumbledore's Army

PATRONUS:
Jack Russell terrier

Actor Rupert Grint felt an affinity to Ron Weasley from his first reading of the Harry Potter novels. "We had a lot of little things in common. Obviously, I'm a ginger," Grint says with a laugh. "We both come from large families. I felt my family was quite similar to the Weasleys, really." After a series of auditions, Grint landed the part, but can't remember his reaction when he got the news. "It's not like I blacked out or anything. I guess it's weird but the only thing I can remember is an intense happiness."

Judianna Makovsky's approach to the character of Ron helped define the look of the Weasley family. "Because his family isn't as rich as other wizarding families," explains Makovsky, "and they're a bit like outcasts because of that, I tried to make his clothes a little stranger than everybody else's. His mother likes to—and really needs to—make all of his clothing. He wore a lot of knitted sweaters that looked a little off, that weren't perfect for him." One clothing tradition became the "initial" sweater that Molly Weasley would give as a present every Christmas.

INSET: *Ron Weasley dressed in a special Molly Weasley creation—the ubiquitous initialed Christmas sweater in* Harry Potter and the Sorcerer's Stone; *OPPOSITE:* Rupert Grint in a publicity photo for Harry Potter and the Deathly Hallows – Part 1; *TOP:* Hermione and Ron on their way to Hogsmeade in Harry Potter and the Prisoner of Azkaban. Ron's sweater is more classic Molly Weasley; *RIGHT: Sketch of Ron's unique dress robes for the Yule Ball in* Harry Potter and the Goblet of Fire. *Costume design by Jany Temime, illustration by Mauricio Carneiro.*

LEAKY + GREEN
COULDRON

SC. 82
RON

D12

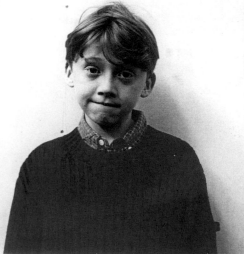

"I'm Ron, by the way. Ron Weasley."

Ron Weasley, *Harry Potter and the Sorcerer's Stone*

Jany Temime counts Ron as possibly her favorite character to dress. "We would laugh every year when we put his costumes together. We would think, that's so awful. You must always wear what Mom gives you," she continues. "But his mom has bad taste, so Ron is very unlucky. His mom has *really bad* taste. But I think he carries it off. Rupert wore everything with one hundred percent sincerity, and he wore it beautifully. He's so likeable, we don't worry about liking what he wears. When he got a bit older, she stopped making them, thank goodness. But he could never really get rid of the style in him."

Being a family of gingers, Temime was resolute about her color palette for Ron and his family. "It was always orange-y, brownish, greenish, that was the color of the Weasleys." In addition to the colors, Temime often used plaids, checks, and stripes to give the clothes a sense of texture, and sometimes combined all of these in the same outfit.

OPPOSITE TOP: *Costume possibilities reflect the Weasley color palette in* Harry Potter and the Prisoner of Azkaban; OPPOSITE BOTTOM: *Continuity shots for* Harry Potter and the Sorcerer's Stone; LEFT: *Rupert Grint on the set of* Harry Potter and the Half-Blood Prince; BELOW: *Ron and his father, Arthur (Mark Williams), showcase Temime's penchant for using checks and patterns to create textures,* Harry Potter and the Deathly Hallows – Part 1.

RON'S WAND

Ron Weasley's first wand, a simple baton style, was broken by the Whomping Willow in *Harry Potter and the Chamber of Secrets*. His second wand echoes the Weasley aesthetic with a rustic interpretation. "It's slightly similar to Harry's," says Pierre Bohanna, "but not quite so refined. It's a bit more like a root that's been whittled quickly." The wands used by the actors were molded from wood, but created in resin. "The trouble is," explains Bohanna, "actual wood wands would be dangerous to use. If they fell, they'd split and shatter. And, wood, by its nature, would be affected by humidity, heat, and cold, and it could bend, buckle, or break, so it's not a practical material to use day to day."

TOP: *Ron Weasley's reaction to his mother's Howler as visualized by Adam Brockbank for* Harry Potter and the Chamber of Secrets; RIGHT: *Ron and Harry on the Hogwarts Express before changing into their robes in* Harry Potter and the Sorcerer's Stone; OPPOSITE LEFT: *Rupert Grint portrays the new Gryffindor Keeper in a publicity photo for* Harry Potter and the Half-Blood Prince.

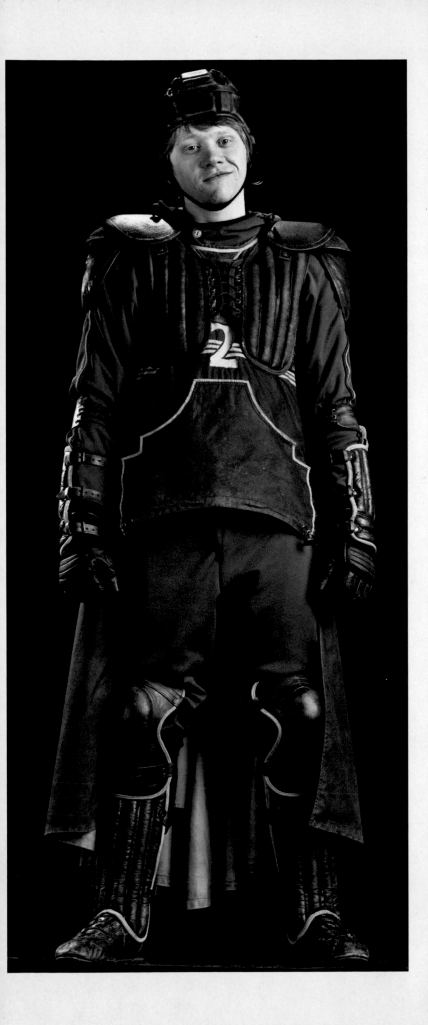

The Biggest Bruiser

In the early days of filming the Harry Potter films, Daniel Radcliffe and Rupert Grint often competed to see who could have the biggest cut or bruise applied by the makeup team, recalls Amanda Knight, "which seemed like a good idea at the time to them. But as scenes often took weeks or months to film, they'd begin to wish they'd opted for a smaller makeup job!"

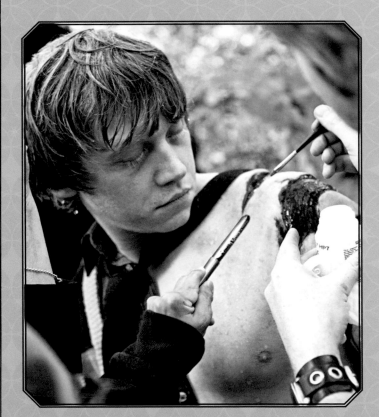

TOP: *A scratched and bruised Harry Potter after a Quidditch match in* Harry Potter and the Prisoner of Azkaban*; ABOVE: Rupert Grint has his splinched shoulder touched up in* Harry Potter and the Deathly Hallows – Part 1.

Hermione Granger

"When I was being interviewed during early films," says actress Emma Watson, who plays Hermione Granger, "I would say I'm not like her at all, and try to convince everyone that I wasn't. I was absolutely adamant about that. But at school, I was very academic and very insecure and a bit of a tomboy. I basically *was* her, to be fair! And I think that helped me 'get' her. I believe I'm a bit more sporty than she is, but I've come to accept our similarities."

Judianna Makovsky's take for Hermione Granger's wardrobe referenced the idea of classic British clothing for the few times she is not wearing her Hogwarts robes. "We looked for pleated skirts, knee socks, lovely handmade Fair Isle sweaters," recalls Makovsky, "harking back to the thirties and forties British boarding school. I think this look seemed most appropriate for her, especially as she seemed so concerned about fitting in."

In the books, Hermione is noted for having buck teeth, and so the makeup department created a set of false teeth for her to wear in *Harry Potter and the Sorcerer's Stone*. "They looked a little silly and they affected Emma's speech but we decided to try them on the first day of shooting," recalls director Chris Columbus.

FIRST APPEARANCE:
Harry Potter and the Sorcerer's Stone

ADDITIONAL APPEARANCES:
Harry Potter and the Chamber of Secrets
Harry Potter and the Prisoner of Azkaban
Harry Potter and the Goblet of Fire
Harry Potter and the Order of the Phoenix
Harry Potter and the Half-Blood Prince
Harry Potter and the Deathly Hallows – Part 1
Harry Potter and the Deathly Hallows – Part 2

HOUSE:
Gryffindor

OCCUPATION:
Hogwarts Student

MEMBER OF:
Dumbledore's Army

PATRONUS:
Otter

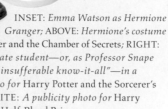

INSET: *Emma Watson as Hermione Granger;* ABOVE: *Hermione's costume for* Harry Potter and the Chamber of Secrets; RIGHT: *The consummate student—or, as Professor Snape calls her, "the insufferable know-it-all"—in a publicity photo for* Harry Potter and the Sorcerer's Stone; OPPOSITE: *A publicity photo for* Harry Potter and the Half-Blood Prince.

"I'm going to bed before either of you come up with another clever idea to get us killed, or worse, expelled."

Hermione Granger, *Harry Potter and the Sorcerer's Stone* film

After the day's rushes were viewed, it was immediately decided to scrap that idea. Sharp viewers can see the only use of this attempt in the last scene of *Harry Potter and the Sorcerer's Stone*, as the three children board the Hogwarts Express.

Director Alfonso Cuarón's approach that the growing kids should express themselves through more contemporary clothing was very much appreciated by Watson. "Thank goodness we didn't have to wear the uniforms all the time," she admits. "I was out of those itchy sweaters! I'm in jeans. Even the hair has been toned down a bit, and a little shorter. But I think this makes it much more contemporary, and shows that we're becoming teenagers." Still, Jany Temime always believed that Hermione was much more concerned about her studies than her clothes. "I dressed Hermione as a girl who felt her best asset was her brain, and wasn't worried about making an effort with her clothes," she says. "She's very busy with her studies and very down-to-earth in what she wears. She may be dressed very practically, but always looks lovely because Emma Watson is a beautiful girl." Temime chose a palette of pinks and grays for the simple, practical outfits Hermione wore. Through the course of the Harry Potter films, Temime recognized that the actress had not only a great fashion sense herself, but also knew what was good for her character. She realized at a certain point that Watson was putting the look of her part before her own personal tastes. "She would say, 'Of course it's not my taste, but Hermione would wear that, you know.'"

TOP: *Early behind-the-scenes shots of Emma Watson as Hermione Granger in* Harry Potter and the Sorcerer's Stone; LEFT: *Sketches of the girls' uniforms by Mauricio Caneiro;* OPPOSITE: *Adam Brockbank's artwork of Hermione after she takes the Polyjuice Potion in* Harry Potter and the Chamber of Secrets.

TOP LEFT AND RIGHT: *Whether in her robes at Hogwarts in* Harry Potter and the Half-Blood Prince *or in Muggle clothes in* Harry Potter and the Half-Blood Prince, *Emma Watson had an intuitive sense of what her character would wear and how she would wear it;* ABOVE: *Hermione places the Time-Turner around Harry's neck in* Harry Potter and the Prisoner of Azkaban. OPPOSITE LEFT AND RIGHT: *Dressed up for the Yule Ball in* Harry Potter and the Goblet of Fire, *and for the Weasley wedding in* Deathly Hallows – Part 1.

Prior to *Harry Potter and the Goblet of Fire*, hair and makeup artists Amanda Knight and Eithne Fennell were strict about not putting lip color or any other noticeable makeup on her, as her character needed to appear appreciably different for the Yule Ball. Until that point, Hermione had, as Fennel describes, "geeky" hair. And, "Hermione only became interested in her clothes when she became interested in Ron," Temime laughs. In *Harry Potter and the Half-Blood Prince*, "Hermione sees that Ron is getting lots of attention from other girls. So I think she tries harder to be more feminine. Not frilly, but she is making more of an effort." "I don't think Hermione ever knew how to apply makeup or do her hair particularly well," says Watson. "That was always an untapped universe to her."

HERMIONE'S WAND

Hermione Granger's wand was hand carved from a type of wood called "London plain," similar to limewood. It's a hardwood so it allows fine details to be carved into it. The wand was gently stained to highlight the ivy-like growth that twists all the way up to its tip. Emma Watson particularly enjoyed the wand battles. "The choreography doesn't look like anything else," she said about the Ministry battle in *Harry Potter and the Order of the Phoenix*. "It's like everything rolled into one: sword-fighting, karate, dances moves, even a bit of *The Matrix*. Putting all these together makes for something that's a completely original art form, very elegant and poised." Watson felt the scene was the first time "you really become aware and impressed by what wizards are capable of doing."

NEVILLE LONGBOTTOM

FIRST APPEARANCE:
Harry Potter and the Sorcerer's Stone

ADDITIONAL APPEARANCES:
Harry Potter and the Chamber of Secrets
Harry Potter and the Prisoner of Azkaban
Harry Potter and the Goblet of Fire
Harry Potter and the Order of the Phoenix
Harry Potter and the Half-Blood Prince
Harry Potter and the Deathly Hallows – Part 1
Harry Potter and the Deathly Hallows – Part 2

HOUSE:
Gryffindor

OCCUPATION:
Hogwarts Student

MEMBER OF:
Dumbledore's Army

C ostumes and makeup are of the utmost importance," says actor Matthew Lewis, who plays Neville Longbottom. "When you're an actor, it helps to get you into the role. When you look in the mirror and you don't see yourself, when you see the character, it really helps you to focus. I appreciate all that's been done in terms of getting me into the right frame of mind."

Neville Longbottom is not only gawky and insecure, he is pudgy and bucktoothed, with ears that come forward like Dumbo's. "For most of the films, I've worn a piece of molded plastic that makes my ears stick out. I wear false teeth that are crooked. And I wear a fat suit, all of which I think I should mention at the start of every interview I give." One cast member was completely unaware of what Lewis did to transform into his character. When Jessie Cave, who plays Lavender Brown, came back for *Harry Potter and the Deathly Hallows – Part 2*, she made a comment to a member of the costume department about how impressed she was at Matthew Lewis's weight loss. The costumer informed her that Lewis wore a fat suit for the part. "I think she's been apologizing to me every time she sees me now," Lewis says with a laugh. "She told me that she thought that my weight just fluctuated up and down!"

Lewis stopped wearing the false teeth and protruding ears in *Harry Potter and the Order of the Phoenix*, and lost the fat suit for *Harry Potter and the Deathly Hallows – Part 1* and *Part 2*. "I was lucky that I could take everything off at the end of the day," observes Lewis, "but in *Deathly Hallows – Part 2*,

INSET: *Matthew Lewis as Neville Longbottom;* TOP: *Neville is seen onto the Hogwarts Express by his grandmother (Leila Hoffman) in* Harry Potter and the Sorcerer's Stone; RIGHT: *Neville in* Sorcerer's Stone *with buck teeth and padded waist;* OPPOSITE: *A publicity photo from* Harry Potter and the Deathly Hallows – Part 2.

Neville's slimmed down. We're trying to suggest he's living underground at Hogwarts, and he's been this resistance leader. So he's not had time to eat, and he's been stressing out." There was another prosthetic that included a headpiece Lewis wore during the battle for Hogwarts, as he's received a wound. "The first week, it was really enjoyable. I thought, 'This is fun! This is great.' Then it gets pretty boring. The novelty definitely wears off."

Other than physical, Lewis observed another great transformation in not only his character, but himself. "When I started, I wasn't that far detached from Neville. I was quite shy and definitely not the top of my class and I didn't want to speak up in a crowded room, but as he started growing confidence in his own abilities, so did I. Of course, we bring our own life experiences into a role, but I think now as much as there is Matt Lewis in Neville, I'm glad to think some Neville has found its way into Matt Lewis."

NEVILLE'S WAND

Neville Longbottom's wand is defined by a spiral on its dark wood handle that creates a three-part twist. Matthew Lewis (Neville) remembers pretending to play a "Harry Potter" game after he read *Harry Potter and the Sorcerer's Stone*. "A friend and I put on bathrobes to be our school robes," he explains, "and then we went outside, got some twigs to be our wands, and fired spells at each other all day." Draftsman Hattie Storey would agree with his choice of the natural material. "I always thought the more successful wands were those that looked like they were half-whittled out of a bit of root. They look quite magical, I think, and mysterious."

TOP: *A pajama-clad Neville is rendered immobile by* Petrificus Totalus *in* Harry Potter and the Sorcerer's Stone*; ABOVE: Practicing the Disarming Charm in* Harry Potter and the Order of the Phoenix*; RIGHT: Helping Harry by providing gillyweed for the second task in* Harry Potter and the Goblet of Fire*; OPPOSITE TOP: Visual development artist Andrew Williamson paints a lyrical picture of Neville practicing the waltz atop a Hogwarts roof in* Goblet of Fire*; OPPOSITE BOTTOM: Neville brings Hermione, Ron, and Harry to the Room of Requirement in* Harry Potter and the Deathly Hallows – Part 2.

"Why is it always me?"

Neville Longbottom, *Harry Potter and the Chamber of Secrets*

FRED & GEORGE WEASLEY

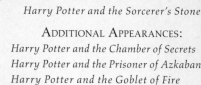

James and Oliver Phelps, who play Fred and George Weasley, respectively, were fans of the Harry Potter books from the start but admit that when their mother told them about an open casting call for *Harry Potter and the Sorcerer's Stone*, they were more interested in having a day off from school. "We said, 'Okay, yeah, all right, if we *have* to,'" recalls James. At the audition, they realized that they were the only twins not wearing identical clothing, so ran to the nearest shop to find matching shirts. Then none of their friends believed them when they were eventually cast as the Weasley twins until they turned up at school one day with ginger-colored hair. The final hitch was when they showed up for the first script read-through. "When we got there," recalls Oliver, "we went to one of the associate directors to ask who was playing who?" "We had gotten two scripts," James continues, "but no one had told us who was Fred and who was George! Finally, someone from casting told us who was who, but we were never sure if it was planned or just a quick decision."

When not in Hogwarts robes, Fred and George were dressed identically in *Harry Potter and the Sorcerer's Stone* and *Harry Potter and the Chamber of Secrets*, holding up their end of the Weasley homemade style. Jany Temime continued the tradition until *Harry Potter and the Order of the Phoenix*, when it's clear that the twins are establishing their own identities as they begin the process of becoming entrepreneurs. In addition to wearing their school clothing differently, following Temime's approach that this was a way for the students to express their personalities, she dressed the twins in similar shirts and sweaters, but in complementary colors.

FIRST APPEARANCE:
Harry Potter and the Sorcerer's Stone

ADDITIONAL APPEARANCES:
Harry Potter and the Chamber of Secrets
Harry Potter and the Prisoner of Azkaban
Harry Potter and the Goblet of Fire
Harry Potter and the Order of the Phoenix
Harry Potter and the Half-Blood Prince
Harry Potter and the Deathly Hallows – Part 1
Harry Potter and the Deathly Hallows – Part 2

HOUSE:
Gryffindor

OCCUPATION:
Hogwarts Students, Gryffindor Beaters, owners of Weasleys' Wizard Wheezes

MEMBER OF:
Dumbledore's Army

INSETS: *The Weasley twins: George (Oliver Phelps, top) and Fred (James Phelps, center);* ABOVE: *Fred and George follow their older brother Percy (Christopher Rankin) onto Platform 9 ¾ in* Harry Potter and the Sorcerer's Stone; RIGHT: *Jany Temime felt the twins "branded" their look in* Harry Potter and the Half-Blood Prince, *illustration by Mauricio Carneiro;* OPPOSITE: *A publicity shot for* Half-Blood Prince.

> ### "Wow, we're identical!"
>
> Fred and George Weasley, *Harry Potter*
> *and the Deathly Hallows – Part 1*

For *Harry Potter and the Half-Blood Prince*, as the twins have now created their own business, Weasleys' Wizard Wheezes, Temime saw them as establishing their own "brand." Their three-piece suits still match, but their shirts and shoes contrast, as well as their light-up ties. The suits were made by a London tailor, who was asked to provide a special pocket in the suit. "There's a little secret compartment inside the waistcoat," explains Oliver, "that holds a battery, which is how we control the flashing tie." Overall, Temime wanted them to be chic. "They have their own shop, so they have money, so they can be stylish. In their own way, of course, but stylish."

In *Harry Potter and the Deathly Hallows – Part 1*, George Weasley loses an ear during the transfer of Harry to The Burrow and so Oliver Phelps needed to have a life cast done of his head, "The only time I've felt claustrophobic," he admits. "We thought that it would be, like, six blue dots around his ear," says James, "and the rest would be done by the computer, but it wasn't." Three prosthetic pieces were created for the effect, underneath a bandage and a wig that Oliver wore. At one point, he and director David Yates came up with the idea that "Maybe George had put a cartoonish-type ear on, and we had a competition for ideas, which Rupert won. We didn't do it, but I think maybe George didn't want to fix it, for the jokes. He did get to stick a toothbrush in the ear." "Well," teases James, "there isn't much brain there to keep the thing from falling out."

OPPOSITE TOP: *The Weasley twins' suits for* Harry Potter and the Half-Blood Prince *as designed by Jany Temime, illustration by Mauricio Carneiro;* OPPOSITE BOTTOM: *Rupert Grint and his movie brothers Oliver and James Phelps share a laugh at King's Cross Station behind the scenes on* Harry Potter and the Order of the Phoenix; TOP: *The Weasleys enter their tent at the 422nd Quidditch World Cup;* ABOVE: *Taking a bet on the first task of the Triwizard Tournament in* Harry Potter and the Goblet of Fire, *Fred wears a Molly-knitted cap and sweater.* RIGHT: *Dumbledore's Army practices in a scene from* Harry Potter and the Order of the Phoenix.

FRED'S & GEORGE'S WANDS

The wands for Weasley twins Fred and George couldn't be more different. George's wand resembles a broomstick. "The *newest* style broomstick," says Oliver Phelps (George). "It's woven around at the end, and there's even a kind of saddle on it." "Mine has more like a pine cone at the end," says James Phelps (Fred). Several versions of each wand were made for different uses. "I know I had three," says James. "One that was like a hard rubber, and the other two were wood. I know they were wood because I broke both of them." "Not while shooting any action," Oliver adds. "It was on a photo shoot!"

Ginny Weasley

When asked if she would ever dress like her character, Ginny Weasley, actress Bonnie Wright smiles. "I think there are some quite unusual and different outfits that she has, but I don't think I would particularly wear the clothes that she wears. That's probably kind of helpful for me, because when I put them on it's a contrast to what I usually wear. It's a step to becoming the character."

"Of course there is a lot of knitting and crochet in Ginny's wardrobes," say Jany Temime. "For a long time, you could see that the mother was making clothes for the daughter. But for *Harry Potter and the Goblet of Fire*, we thought, no more. Ginny has decided to buy her own clothes. We wanted Ginny to change." Bonnie Wright agreed with the change. "Obviously, as she becomes older and more outgoing and confident in herself, she probably tries to tear away from the Weasley look. She does become less orange and less woolly." As Ginny matured, Temime dressed her in a different palette than her brothers, tending toward pinks instead of oranges, and used greens and browns that were dark and muted. Girlish jewelry and hair accessories disappeared. "Her wardrobe needed to reflect the delicate balance of a growing girl," explains Temime.

Bonnie Wright agrees that for Ginny's growing relationship with Harry, they needed her look to develop. "Because she was raised with all these older brothers, she's never really been a 'girly' girl. But at the Christmas party in *Harry Potter and the Half-Blood Prince*, you can see she's growing up, becoming a young woman. And it's obvious that Harry is seeing her in a different way, he's realizing his interest in her. So I think she's got to do something for him to recognize his new feelings."

PREVIOUS PAGES: *Artwork by Andrew Williamson for* Harry Potter and the Order of the Phoenix; INSET: *Bonnie Wright as Ginny Weasley;* OPPOSITE FAR LEFT: *Wright sports a muted color palette in a publicity photo for* Harry Potter and the Half-Blood Prince; OPPOSITE BOTTOM: *Harry Potter asks the Weasleys for directions to Platform 9 ¾ in* Harry Potter and the Sorcerer's Stone; ABOVE: *Ginny before her first kiss with Harry in the Room of Requirement in* Half-Blood Prince; LEFT: *Bonnie Wright poses in her Hogwarts robes in a publicity photo for* Harry Potter and the Chamber of Secrets.

FIRST APPEARANCE:
Harry Potter and the Sorcerer's Stone

ADDITIONAL APPEARANCES:
Harry Potter and the Chamber of Secrets
Harry Potter and the Prisoner of Azkaban
Harry Potter and the Goblet of Fire
Harry Potter and the Order of the Phoenix
Harry Potter and the Half-Blood Prince
Harry Potter and the Deathly Hallows – Part 1
Harry Potter and the Deathly Hallows – Part 2

HOUSE:
Gryffindor

OCCUPATION:
Hogwarts Student, Gryffindor Chaser

MEMBER OF:
Dumbledore's Army

PATRONUS:
Horse

GINNY'S WAND

Ginny Weasley's all-black wand features a swirl on the handle and a short studded section that creates a transition from the handle to the shaft. While filming *Order of the Phoenix*, Bonnie Wright noted a clear difference in the wand styles displayed by the actors during the battle in the Ministry. "Obviously, everyone holds their pen differently," she explains, "so it's kind of the same in the way you hold your wand. And when we chose our wands, before filming *Prisoner of Azkaban*, I think it was based on which one felt right in our character's hands as much as for the look."

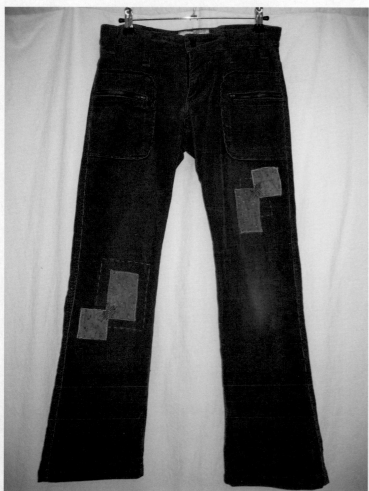

INSET: *Ginny Weasley practices her spells in* Harry Potter and the Order of the Phoenix; OPPOSITE TOP: *Bonnie Wright wears a rosier version of the Weasley palette in a publicity photo from* Harry Potter and the Goblet of Fire; OPPOSITE BOTTOM: *Harry Potter and Ginny in the new Quidditch practice wear for tryouts in* Harry Potter and the Half-Blood Prince; TOP AND ABOVE: *Homemade with love—a knitted hair tie and patched pants worn in* Half-Blood Prince.

Non-Wizard Wear

After Harry Potter and the Prisoner of Azkaban, *the students began to frequently dress in contemporary clothing. Brand logos were still not allowed, and Jany Temime considered the characters' proximities to current trends. "Harry and Hermione are more aware of fashion in the Muggle world," she explains, "while Ginny and Ron are not, and their choice of clothes would reflect that, as well the influence of their own wizardy culture." To her, the challenge was to "keep them in character, dress them in a cool, modern way, and still have something magical about it." Ginny and the other kids' "Muggle" clothes were purchased at London shops, but typically changed. "Whatever we buy, it's new and it has to look like it's been worn, so we have to create that." At least thirty percent of these clothes were purchased, always in multiples, and then customized with added embellishments and alterations to sleeves and collars, and different buttons and fastenings.*

TOP AND ABOVE: *While their clothes might have come from "Muggle" stores, Jany Temime's ensembles still broadcast "We're Weasleys" for Ginny in* Harry Potter and the Order of the Phoenix *and Ron and Ginny in* Harry Potter and the Goblet of Fire.

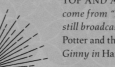

DRACO MALFOY

During his audition for *Harry Potter and the Sorcerer's Stone*, actor Tom Felton knew he shouldn't reveal that he wasn't particularly familiar with the Harry Potter books. "One of the first things they asked at the audition was 'What is your favorite scene in *Sorcerer's Stone*?' I was in a row of about seven actors, and the guy next to me said, 'Oh, Gringotts, I love the trolls.' When I was asked, I just said the same thing as him. 'I love the trolls, they're brilliant.' And I think Chris Columbus saw through that straight away." Felton initially auditioned for the parts of Harry and Ron ("and Hermione!" he quips) before he was cast as the hero's silver-haired enemy.

For the look of Draco Malfoy, son of a very rich pure-blood wizard family, Judianna Makovsky felt that it would be more effective to keep things simple and not let Draco's evilness be eclipsed by his clothing. One part of his look that did stand out was his white-blond hair. "My hair was obviously slicked back in the early years; they used a *lot* of hair gel," Felton recalls. As the films continued, the haircut became more natural, but for *Harry Potter and the Goblet of Fire*, "I wore a wig," Felton admits, "because I was getting tired of dyeing my hair blond every week, and they allowed me to do this. But I realized it looked better when it was blond for real, and that dyeing it wasn't so much of a problem for me when the result was worth it."

There were several occasions for Malfoy to show off his family's wealth—in *Harry Potter and the Prisoner of Azkaban*, during the trip to Hogsmeade, his clothes included a fur hat and designer coat that contrasted sharply with Ron's and Hermione's plain homemade wear, and his tuxedo robes in *Harry Potter and the*

FIRST APPEARANCE:
Harry Potter and the Sorcerer's Stone

ADDITIONAL APPEARANCES:
Harry Potter and the Chamber of Secrets
Harry Potter and the Prisoner of Azkaban
Harry Potter and the Goblet of Fire
Harry Potter and the Order of the Phoenix
Harry Potter and the Half-Blood Prince
Harry Potter and the Deathly Hallows – Part 1
Harry Potter and the Deathly Hallows – Part 2

HOUSE:
Slytherin

OCCUPATION:
Hogwarts Student, Slytherin Seeker

MEMBER OF:
The Inquisitorial Squad,
Death Eaters

INSET: *Tom Felton as Draco Malfoy;* RIGHT AND OPPOSITE: *Tom Felton in publicity photos for* Harry Potter and the Sorcerer's Stone *and* Harry Potter and the Half-Blood Prince; ABOVE: *Detention in the Forbidden Forest.*

"*My father will hear about this!*"

Draco Malfoy, *Harry Potter and the Goblet of Fire*

Goblet of Fire were top of the line. But it is in *Harry Potter and the Half-Blood Prince* that Draco became a true fashion plate. "Draco has made the decision to follow his father with the goal of becoming a Death Eater," Jany Temime explains. "He's dressed in a tailored black suit more often than his school robes because we wanted to show that he thinks of himself as already being on his way out of school. That he is consciously separating himself from being a student." Through the course of the films, Tom Felton often received fan mail asking for him to put a different color into his wardrobe, but teases that, knowing his character, "There's no occasion where black doesn't fit in as far as Draco's concerned."

DRACO'S WAND

The simple design of Draco Malfoy's blunt-tipped wand was crafted from a light brown Mexican rosewood attached to a jet-black ebony handle. Draco was also briefly the master of Dumbledore's wand, after *Half-Blood Prince*, but he then lost his own wand to Harry Potter in *Deathly Hallows – Part 1*. Tom Felton is one of many actors who would choose his wand to take home as a souvenir of his time on the Harry Potter films. "Warwick Davis [Professor Flitwick] and I had a conversation about this one day," Felton recalls. "We asked, if we could take an item or two, what would we take? Both our first thoughts were our wands."

OPPOSITE TOP: *Draco Malfoy awaits the Care of Magical Creatures class in* Harry Potter and the Prisoner of Azkaban *carrying his textbook and a personalized leather book bag;* OPPOSITE BOTTOM: *On a Hogsmeade visit, accompanied by Crabbe (Jamie Waylett), Draco keeps warm in a fur hat and leather gloves in* Prisoner of Azkaban; TOP: *Draco works on the Vanishing Cabinet in* Harry Potter and the Half-Blood Prince; ABOVE: *Slytherins Gregory Goyle (Josh Herdman) and Blaise Zabini (Louis Cordice) flank Draco during a fiery confrontation in* Harry Potter and the Deathly Hallows – Part 2.

LUNA LOVEGOOD

Luna Lovegood might be considered "different" in comparison to her classmates at Hogwarts, but Jany Temime wanted to make sure that Luna did not appear freakish. "She may dress a bit more 'wizardy' than the other girls, but it's in Luna's personality to do that. She is clearly a girl with her own tastes and her own hobbies, which include making her own jewelry." Actress Evanna Lynch's knowledge of the character was a valuable resource to the designer. When Temime made a pair of red radish-shaped beaded earrings for her, Lynch insisted that the color was supposed to be orange (and they were actually Dirigible Plums). "She was very specific about a few things that were from her character," recalls Temime. "There was the Butterbeer-cap necklace, and shoes with strawberries on them. In fact, we put strawberries everywhere throughout her clothes because she liked strawberries." Lynch herself made the beaded hare ring that Luna wears to Professor Slughorn's Christmas party in *Harry Potter and the Half-Blood Prince*, as well as designing the lion hat she wears as a supporter of the Gryffindor Quidditch team.

Luna's mismatched outfits were colored dominantly in purples and blues, and the fabrics often featured animals or natural elements that added to their folk art feel. Jany Temime always considered that Luna lived in "her own homemade world. You felt she was a kid who collected insects or animals. She has an approach to the world that nobody else has. And I always wanted to reflect that in her clothing. I think it mattered."

INSET: *Evanna Lynch as Luna Lovegood;* RIGHT: *Lynch poses in a costume reference photo for* Harry Potter and the Order of the Phoenix; BELOW AND OPPOSITE LEFT: *Costume sketches showcase the uniqueness of Luna's wardrobe in designs by Jany Temime, sketches by Mauricio Carneiro;* OPPOSITE RIGHT: *Luna's Gryffindor-supporting hat as envisioned by Adam Brockbank for* Harry Potter and the Half-Blood Prince.

FIRST APPEARANCE:
Harry Potter and the Order of the Phoenix

ADDITIONAL APPEARANCES:
Harry Potter and the Half-Blood Prince
Harry Potter and the Deathly Hallows – Part 1
Harry Potter and the Deathly Hallows – Part 2

HOUSE:
Ravenclaw

OCCUPATION:
Hogwarts Student

MEMBER OF:
Dumbledore's Army

PATRONUS:
Hare

> *"You're just as sane as I am."*
>
> Luna Lovegood, *Harry Potter and the Order of the Phoenix*

Harry Potter producer David Heyman and director David Yates both have said of the actress, "Evanna *is* Luna." Lynch agrees, having felt an immediate connection to the character when she read *Harry Potter and the Order of the Phoenix*. One significant difference, Lynch will point out, is that she is probably more determined than Luna. Lynch waited in line for four hours as one of fifteen thousand young women to audition for the part in open casting calls that took place across the United Kingdom.

LUNA'S WAND

Like Ron Weasley, Luna Lovegood had two wands. Her first wand was a baton-style, with a vine featuring acorns that spiraled around it. For the scene where Luna first learns to cast a Patronus charm, in *Harry Potter and the Order of the Phoenix*, "I was a bit disappointed," actress Evanna Lynch recalls. "I said *Expecto Patronum* and not a thing came out of my wand, you know." This wand was confiscated by Death Eaters in *Harry Potter and the Deathly Hallows – Part 1*. During their imprisonment, it's reasoned, Ollivander fashioned her a new wand, of a darker wood, with a long tulip-like flower as the handle.

Chapter 2

HOGWARTS STAFF

Professor Dumbledore

When actor Richard Harris visited Judianna Makovsky about his costumes as Professor Albus Percival Wulfric Brian Dumbledore for *Harry Potter and the Sorcerer's Stone*, she showed him some preliminary sketches for the headmaster. "He stared at them for a while, and then said 'Thank you. Thank you, now I know what my character is,' and that was it. Richard Harris made it simple." Makovsky had met with author J.K. Rowling prior to this, who told the designer that Dumbledore liked clothes and had a certain amount of personal vanity. "She was insistent that he was, as I would describe, a clothes-horse." Makovsky employed two embroiderers, who also do work for Queen Elizabeth, to embellish his robes, one of which took eight weeks to decorate with Celtic symbols. "I think he changed clothes more than anyone else in the film," she says. "But Richard was a delight to work with." In addition to the handwork, the fabrics were silk-screened and appliqued so the material did not look "manufactured." During filming, Harris spent several hours in the makeup chair being tressed in long white hair and an equally white knee-length beard, which chief makeup artist Amanda Knight would tie up with ribbons during food breaks.

For *Harry Potter and the Chamber of Secrets*, when Harry is introduced to Fawkes in the headmaster's office, costume designer Lindy Hemming created the robe Dumbledore wears using antique pieces of fabric and cut-outs from an old tapestry. Dumbledore also required a costume for scenes that take place fifty years earlier. Michael O'Connor, associate costume designer, felt that Dumbledore's wardrobe needed only to be simpler.

FIRST APPEARANCE:
Harry Potter and the Sorcerer's Stone

ADDITIONAL APPEARANCES:
Harry Potter and the Chamber of Secrets
Harry Potter and the Prisoner of Azkaban
Harry Potter and the Goblet of Fire
Harry Potter and the Order of the Phoenix
Harry Potter and the Half-Blood Prince
Harry Potter and the Deathly Hallows – Part 1
Harry Potter and the Deathly Hallows – Part 2

HOUSE:
Gryffindor

OCCUPATION:
Hogwarts Headmaster

MEMBER OF:
Order of the Phoenix

PATRONUS:
Phoenix

PRECEDING PAGE: *Professors McGonagall (Maggie Smith) and Dumbledore (Michael Gambon) attend the Yule Ball in* Harry Potter and the Goblet of Fire; INSET: *Richard Harris as Albus Dumbledore;* OPPOSITE: *Dumbledore wears the robe that included old tapestry pieces in* Harry Potter and the Chamber of Secrets; ABOVE: *With Harry in the headmaster's office in* Chamber of Secrets; RIGHT: *Costume design by Judianna Makovsky for one of Dumbledore's robes. Sketch by Laurent Guinci.*

"We kept the same colors and textures, just not as elaborate as they are when he's the headmaster of Hogwarts. So we kept the wardrobe in purples and rich browns and golds, and made the silhouette slightly smaller and less exaggerated." Sadly, after the second film was completed, actor Richard Harris passed away.

Actor Michael Gambon would now essay the role of Dumbledore. So Jany Temime combined the original concept that the headmaster loved dressing up with the personality of the new actor portraying him. "I felt Dumbledore was somebody who was always moving, somebody who was very spirited, and very sure of himself." Director Alfonso Cuarón agreed, and gave her his own thoughts. "His description was 'old hippie,' but still very chic and with a lot of class. He said that Dumbledore was the sort of man who, when he sat down, everything would fall into place naturally." Temime dressed the headmaster in layers of tie-dyed silks that moved with him, and changed out high, pointed wizard hats for a style that resembles Victorian "Oriental" tasseled smoking caps. He was additionally adorned with Celtic-design rings, and often tied his beard with a thin chain. Temime was also charged with dressing a much younger Dumbledore, when he visits the orphan Tom Riddle in *Harry Potter and the Half-Blood Prince*, and it's clear that he enjoyed wearing the flamboyant clothes of that time.

> *"As long as Dumbledore's around, Harry, you're safe. As long as Dumbledore's around, you can't be touched."*
>
> Hermione Granger, *Harry Potter and the Sorcerer's Stone*

Prior to the events of *Harry Potter and the Half-Blood Prince*, as Dumbledore has been injured in pursuit of a Horcrux and is dealing with the growing power of Voldemort's Dark forces, the beloved headmaster needed to seem more vulnerable. Usually dressed in vibrant hues of purple and lavender, Temime washed out as much color as she could from his robes, and added the effects of damage and dirt that had not been seen before. Amanda Knight was also charged with this different approach. "We made his beard and hair longer and straighter, and whiter than in previous films," Knight explains. "And we removed his hat so that he seemed more naked somehow."

OPPOSITE FAR LEFT: *Robe design by Jany Temime, sketch by Mauricio Carneiro for* Harry Potter and the Half-Blood Prince; OPPOSITE CENTER AND TOP: *Wardrobe for a flashback in* Half-Blood Prince *epitomized the style of the times. Suit design by Jany Temime, sketch by Mauricio Carneiro;* OPPOSITE RIGHT: *Close-ups of embroidery details on one of the robes;* TOP: *An Oriental-style cap;* ABOVE: *As Dumbledore's power was tested, his wardrobe became more gray;* RIGHT: *A costume reference photo for* Half-Blood Prince.

DUMBLEDORE
Quality The Berwick st cloth shop
Width
Metres
Shade
overobe
Quality Whalleys
Width
Metres Silk Twill
Shade
underobe
Quality Zimmer Rohde
Width
Metres
Shade
bib
Quality Nya Nordiska
Width
Metres
Shade
Quality
Width
Metres
Shade
© 1986
Obtainable from stock MORPLAN London W1 & Harlow

DUMBLEDORE'S WAND

When they first fashioned Headmaster Albus Dumbledore's wand, the designers had no idea how important that wand would be to the story. The Elder Wand is made from a piece of English oak, with a bone inlay at the handle decorated with runes. "It's very thin as a wand," says Pierre Bohanna, "but it has these outcrops of nodules every few inches, so it's very recognizable, even from a distance." Bohanna was grateful the wand's design was so distinctive. "Obviously, it's the biggest gun on the set, so to speak. As far as wands are concerned, it's the wand to beat all others."

OPPOSITE PAGE: *A collection of robes designed by Jany Temime,* Harry Potter and the Goblet of Fire. *Sketches by Mauricio Carneiro (top left and right);* Harry Potter and the Prisoner of Azkaban. *Sketch by Laurent Guinci (top center);* Harry Potter and the Order of the Phoenix. *Sketch by Mauricio Carneiro (right);* OPPOSITE LEFT: *Swatches of fabric on a chart used for the costumes designed for* Order of the Phoenix; THIS PAGE: *Daniel Radcliffe and Michael Gambon filming on the Cave set in* Harry Potter and the Half-Blood Prince *(top); Dumbledore in Budleigh Babberton in* Half-Blood Prince *(left).*

RUBEUS HAGRID

Contrary to popular rumor, J.K. Rowling did not write the character of Hagrid with actor Robbie Coltrane in mind. In a conversation with the author, Coltrane was told that the model was a Hell's Angel that Rowling knew. "He was huge and terrifying," Coltrane relates, "but a real gentleman who talked about his garden and his petunias." When the filming of *Harry Potter and the Sorcerer's Stone* was announced, however, Rowling did strongly suggest the Scottish actor for the part.

Once Hagrid was cast, the production team needed to make decisions on how the half-giant would interact with the considerably smaller ensemble. In movies with similar considerations, the characters are placed in digitally, which ultimately complicates filming and visual effects. Creature effects designer Nick Dudman suggested that for the long shots a large double for Hagrid could be used. Concern for finding someone who could fulfill the gigantic proportion required was voiced, but Dudman was nonplussed. "We thought that if we used the tallest person we could find, and then scaled him up via a suit as big as we could go, we could get to a height of about seven foot seven." Martin Bayfield, a six foot ten ex-England rugby player, was hired. "We life-cast both of them," says Dudman, "and then basically constructed a Robbie suit with a static head that Martin would wear." The studio—and Dudman—wasn't completely convinced that it would work until a test that the crew put together for director Chris Columbus and producer David Heyman. Coltrane was filmed in costume and then Bayfield emerged from behind a door, mimicking Coltrane's walk and even imitating lines from a bank commercial Coltrane had recently filmed. Columbus and Heyman—and especially Dudman—were completely enthralled and satisfied with the results. Bayfield did have the opportunity to play Hagrid without the animatronic head, portraying him as a student in *Harry Potter and the Chamber of Secrets.*

FIRST APPEARANCE:
Harry Potter and the Sorcerer's Stone

ADDITIONAL APPEARANCES:
Harry Potter and the Chamber of Secrets
Harry Potter and the Prisoner of Azkaban
Harry Potter and the Goblet of Fire
Harry Potter and the Order of the Phoenix
Harry Potter and the Half-Blood Prince
Harry Potter and the Deathly Hallows – Part 1
Harry Potter and the Deathly Hallows – Part 2

HOUSE:
Gryffindor

OCCUPATION:
Keeper of Keys and Grounds of Hogwarts,
Care of Magical Creatures professor
(from third year)

INSET: *Robbie Coltrane as Rubeus Hagrid;* OPPOSITE: *Coltrane in a publicity photo for* Harry Potter and the Sorcerer's Stone; LEFT: *Hagrid wears heat-protective gloves in* Sorcerer's Stone; RIGHT: *Jany Temime added more functionality to Hagrid's clothes starting with* Harry Potter and the Prisoner of Azkaban. *Costume sketch by Laurent Guinci.*

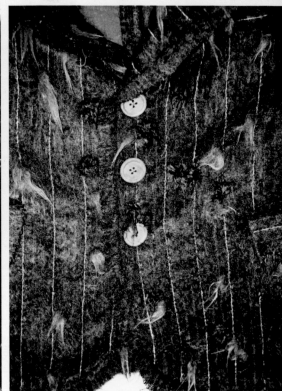

Nick Dudman continued to expand the possibilities of the double's suit, creating a second head that contained animatronic controls for facial movements, and a third head with a voice-activated moving mouth. As the films progressed, Hagrid became more of a digital construct, in order to use Coltrane's performance, but creating a practical half giant that could join the other actors on set inspired the creature effects department to explore other effects practically as well as digitally.

Harry Potter and the Sorcerer's Stone designer Judianna Makovsky needed to consider patterns and accessories for Hagrid's costumes that would seem to appear to be the same size between the actor and his double, as every outfit had to be made twice. Makovsky succeeded at this challenge, and was then immediately presented with another. In the book, Hagrid is described as wearing a moleskin suit. Makovsky asked Rowling if she meant the cotton fabric called moleskin, "or did she mean little moles," Makovsky recalls with a laugh. "And she meant little moles. I thought, well, I can't use real animal skins!" Makovsky purchased fake fur and cut it into mole-shaped pieces in the normal and large sizes, with little feet and heads, and stitched them together to make the coat.

Jany Temime rethought Hagrid's wardrobe when she started on *Harry Potter and the Prisoner of Azkaban*, considering him more of a farmer, tending the forest and teaching about creatures. She provided him with a waistcoat, and thick trousers and boots. In order to accommodate the larger editions of Hagrid's clothes, Temime created her own prints so they could be easily blown up three times bigger. Temime's greatest challenge was the mohair suit Hagrid first wore for Buckbeak's trial; large plugs of mohair needed to be glued onto the double's version to reproduce the same effect as the original fabric. Hagrid wore the hairy suit again for the Yule Ball in *Harry Potter and the Goblet of Fire*, and, "We slicked his own hair down a little when he was flirting," says Eithne Fennell, giving his locks a bit more grooming than usual. "As much as Hagrid can be groomed," adds Amanda Knight.

TOP LEFT TO RIGHT: *Jany Temime designed a furry formal suit for Hagrid, first worn in* Harry Potter and the Prisoner of Azkaban, *as seen in a sketch by Laurent Guinci, a costume reference photo, and a close-up detail;* RIGHT CENTER: *An animatronic head for Hagrid sits next to some Mandrake pots in the creature shop;* RIGHT BOTTOM: *As the new Care of Magical Creatures professor in* Prisoner of Azkaban, *Hagrid needed a more utilitarian coat;* OPPOSITE TOP RIGHT: *Visual development sketches of Hagrid's flute, played in* Harry Potter and the Sorcerer's Stone; OPPOSITE BOTTOM RIGHT: *Early concept art of Hagrid with his umbrella wand, by Paul Catling;* OPPOSITE LEFT: *Hagrid's moleskin coat.*

"There's no Hogwarts without you, Hagrid."

Harry Potter, *Harry Potter and the Chamber of Secrets*

note=
The flutes are printed full sized

Flatten pattern for Hagrid's flute=>

The body and the carved part are stained darker than the pattern.

The 'Owl' has to be carved above a wood knot as if it was standing on a branch tree.

Flatten pattern for Harry's flute=>

HAGRID'S FLUTE.

HARRY'S FLUTE

HAGRID'S WAND

The pieces of Rubeus Hagrid's wand are hidden in a pink umbrella, seen when he uses it to conjure a fire in *Harry Potter and the Sorcerer's Stone*. Just as his costumes needed to be created in two different sizes, a London umbrella maker did the same for Hagrid's umbrella/wand. Because Hagrid is not actually allowed to use his wand, we do not see him raise it in memorial to Dumbledore in *Harry Potter and the Half-Blood Prince*.

ARGUS FILCH

After they read the first few Harry Potter novels, actor David Bradley asked his children which part they thought he should play in the films if he could. "They said I was a natural for Filch," he recalls with a smile, "and I thought, is that how my kids see me? This horrible, greasy, odious, vicious man? Isn't that nice." To their delight, Bradley was asked to audition for the role, and "they were on the ceiling when my agent called and said I was cast."

Before filming started, Bradley had meetings with the costume and makeup departments, who dressed him as, he describes, "A cross between a medieval pickpocket and someone from the Wild West. There was quite a bit of greasy leather and odd bits of fake animals skin in that saggy overcoat." Filch's look is completed with straggly hair extensions, stubble, and a set of repulsive false teeth. Jany Temime adjusted Filch's costume slightly, lessening the oily, ragged look of his vests and tailcoats, and incorporating more of a caretaker's uniform with a color palette that stayed mostly in the brown and gray range. As the films progressed, Filch continued to clean up, even wearing a proper black formal suit at the Yule Ball in *Harry Potter and the Goblet of Fire*, and long quilted armor-like padding in *Harry Potter and the Deathly Hallows – Part 2* during battle scenes.

Over the course of the films, Bradley found it easy to become one with the character. "Once I get into those big, dirty boots and old overcoat, and slide on the teeth, I slip into him and have great fun. I'm not saying I *like* him. I like him as a character but I wouldn't go out for a coffee with him."

FIRST APPEARANCE:
Harry Potter and the Sorcerer's Stone

ADDITIONAL APPEARANCES:
Harry Potter and the Chamber of Secrets
Harry Potter and the Prisoner of Azkaban
Harry Potter and the Goblet of Fire
Harry Potter and the Order of the Phoenix
Harry Potter and the Half-Blood Prince
Harry Potter and the Deathly Hallows – Part 2

OCCUPATION:
Caretaker of Hogwarts

INSET: *David Bradley as Argus Filch*; OPPOSITE: *A publicity photo for* Harry Potter and the Goblet of Fire *displays Filch's formal suit*; ABOVE LEFT AND RIGHT: *The costume breakdown work is evident in this suit ensemble for* Harry Potter and the Prisoner of Azkaban; CENTER RIGHT: *Sketches by Laurent Guinci of Filch's wardrobe designed by Jany Temime for* Harry Potter and the Deathly Hallows – Part 2; RIGHT: *A rune-inscribed whistle from* Harry Potter and the Order of the Phoenix.

"A pity they let the old punishments die."

Argus Filch, *Harry Potter and the Sorcerer's Stone*

Madam Pomfrey

FIRST APPEARANCE:
Harry Potter and the Chamber of Secrets

ADDITIONAL APPEARANCES:
Harry Potter and the Half-Blood Prince
Harry Potter and the Deathly Hallows – Part 2

OCCUPATION:
Hospital Matron

Madam Poppy Pomfrey, first seen in *Harry Potter and the Chamber of Secrets*, is a character that actress Gemma Jones finds "clearly identifiable. I've got lots of fun fan mail from young people who obviously recognize the character that they've read in the books." It's not surprising that an educational institution such as Hogwarts should have its own version of the "school nurse," in this case a matron, and costumer Judianna Makovsky ensured that Madam Pomfrey had her own distinguishable robes. Keeping to the overall choice of a Dickensian-era familiarity for the wizarding wardrobes, Pomfrey wears a uniform that resembles those of the women educated at the Nightingale Training School, established in England in the 1860s. The high starched collar, peaked hat, and long dress/apron combination was believed to be the most protective outfit to wear against disease. Madam Pomfrey's costume includes the nurse's standard equipment of a timepiece, and she wears a pin in the shape of an hourglass.

Madam Pomfrey's uniform was revised for *Harry Potter and the Half-Blood Prince*. Jany Temime kept Pomfrey in a similar color theme—the white and red originated by the American Red Cross brought over the Atlantic by World War I nurses—but gave the outfit more wizardy points. The sleeves are puffed up and the collar comes down in sharp-ending triangles. Temime also provided her with a red-colored cape/cloak combo for outdoor scenes.

INSET: *Gemma Jones as Madam Poppy Pomfrey;* TOP LEFT: *Harry Potter is attended by the hospital matron in* Harry Potter and the Chamber of Secrets; ABOVE AND OPPOSITE: *Pomfrey's outfit was redesigned by Jany Temime as seen in sketches by Mauricio Carneiro and in a scene from* Harry Potter and the Deathly Hallows – Part 2.

POMFREY'S WAND

Madam Pomfrey's baton-style wand is hewed from a dark wood, with a knob shape at the handle. Actress Gemma Jones (Pomfrey) enjoyed her fight scenes for *Harry Potter and the Deathly Hallows – Part 2*. "When filming, it's a bit tame, though the stunt people are flinging themselves onto the ground or hurling themselves in the air," she says. "But when everything's put on, in special effects, with sparks and flashes coming out of our wands, you realize how powerful you are!"

MADAM HOOCH

Although she appears in only *Harry Potter and the Sorcerer's Stone*, Madam Rolanda Hooch, played by actress Zöe Wanamaker, sports an extensive wardrobe. As flying instructor for the students, Hooch wears a starched white shirt and a tie bearing the Hogwarts crest under a heavy wool shift/robe combination. Thick leather gloves and a brass whistle complete the outfit. "I imagined Madam Hooch as sort of a gym instructor," says Judianna Makovsky, "which was confirmed by Jo [Rowling] in our conversations." As depicted in the books, yellow hawk-like eyes were added via contact lenses to the actress, under a spiky hairstyle.

Madam Hooch wears a robe, pants, and guards similar to the players during the Quidditch game as she flies alongside them as referee. The white shirt, tie, and whistle are still present, this time under a sharp buttoned-up vest. Her split-tail black robe, lined in white and decorated in white stripes, bears the Hogwarts crest, and has tied-back sleeves. Hooch also wears a pair of yellow-tinted goggles.

But her flashiest incarnation is seen at the teachers' table in the Great Hall, as she's attired in a showy set of purple robes. This time, her shirt collar points are tipped up, her tie is silk, and her robe has deep purple velvet accents. The vest and sleeves of her dress suit under the robes are bordered in a pattern that mimics licks of flames and gives the illusion of motion even when she's standing still. To top it off—literally—Hooch's pleated hat ends in a purple and white flourish that clearly resembles the brush end of a broomstick.

INSET: *Zöe Wanamaker as Madam Hooch;* ABOVE: *The flight instructor teaches the first years in her training robes in* Harry Potter and the Sorcerer's Stone; RIGHT: *Zöe Wanamaker poses in flame-decorated robes for a publicity photo;* OPPOSITE TOP AND LEFT: *Hooch's referee robes in costume reference shots and worn in a Quidditch game;* OPPOSITE INSET: *Close-up of tie with Hogwarts crest.*

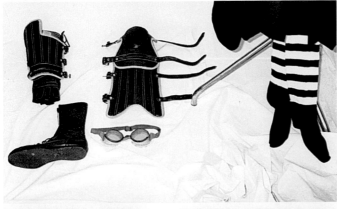

"Welcome to your first flying lesson. Well? What are you waiting for?"

Madam Hooch, *Harry Potter and the Sorcerer's Stone*

PROFESSOR McGONAGALL

"H onestly," says Dame Maggie Smith, who portrays Professor Minerva McGonagall in the Harry Potter film series, "how often do you get to walk around as a wizard with great clothes?" Judianna Makovsky appreciates that the actress offered many ideas about her character and what she should be. "Scottish," Makovsky recalls. "Her name is Scottish, she wanted to *be* Scottish. And dressed, of course, in green."

McGonagall is described in the first novel as being dressed in green but the costume designer struggled as to the hue of the color, and admits that McGonagall's gowns ended up more vibrant than she had originally intended. Makovsky's first designs were rendered in an olive tone, but Dame Maggie felt it needed to be brighter. "She also suggested the Scottish-style wizard version of the deerstalker hat she wears outdoors while watching Quidditch. Even her indoor wizard hat was based on a Scottish tam. We tried to give everything she wore Scottish panache." For *Harry Potter and the Sorcerer's Stone*, Makovsky covered her high-necked black dress with emerald green velvet robes decorated with Celtic symbols, and fashioned her a dressing gown and nightcap out of a tartan plaid.

"Why is it, when something happens, it is always you three?"

Professor McGonagall, *Harry Potter and the Half-Blood Prince*

FIRST APPEARANCE:
Harry Potter and the Sorcerer's Stone

ADDITIONAL APPEARANCES:
Harry Potter and the Chamber of Secrets
Harry Potter and the Prisoner of Azkaban
Harry Potter and the Goblet of Fire
Harry Potter and the Order of the Phoenix
Harry Potter and the Half-Blood Prince
Harry Potter and the Deathly Hallows – Part 2

HOUSE:
Gryffindor

OCCUPATION:
Transfiguration professor,
Head of Gryffindor House

ADDITIONAL SKILL SET:
Animagus

Professor McGonagall's attire frequently features textured fabrics, pleating, and shirring. Buttons, fasteners, and even her jewelry are embellished with traditional Celtic imagery. Jany Temime tailored several of McGonagall's robes with sleeves that were form-fitting to her elbows, then hung down in long points, pleased that the actress "really uses what I give her. She uses the gown, she uses the sleeves. She gives them a nice theatricality." Temime changed the color to a darker, more burnished green, and incorporated what she refers to as "wizardy" elements, adding high points to the shoulders of McGonagall's robes and collars.

INSET: *Dame Maggie Smith as Professor Minerva McGonagall;* OPPOSITE RIGHT: *Preliminary costume designs by Judianna Makovsky, sketched by Laurent Guinci for* Harry Potter and the Sorcerer's Stone; OPPOSITE FAR LEFT: *Smith strikes a professorial pose in a publicity photo for* Sorcerer's Stone; TOP LEFT: *Even McGonagall's bathrobe and sleeping cap, seen in* Sorcerer's Stone, *were infused with Scottish style;* TOP CENTER: *A darker, pointier silhouette was evident in Jany Temime's costume design for* Harry Potter and the Half-Blood Prince. *Sketch by Mauricio Carneiro;* TOP RIGHT: *Judianna Makovsky suggests a different color palette in an early costume sketch by Laurent Guinci;* ABOVE: *Close-up of the Transfiguration professor's boots.*

McGONAGALL'S WAND

Prop modeler Pierre Bohanna describes the design of Minerva McGonagall's wand as "no-nonsense." The sleek black-tipped wand is topped by a carving that seemingly resembles the turned leg on a piece of Victorian furniture, and is finished with a small amber stone at the end of the handle. Maggie Smith thought that her wand battle with Alan Rickman (Severus Snape) in *Harry Potter and the Deathly Hallows – Part 2* would be more physical, and practiced her wand moves as if she was wielding a foil, but realized, "Of course, wands work in a magical way. It can be a long distance from each other when you have a wand."

ABOVE: *Professor McGonagall places the Sorting Hat on Hermione Granger's head in* Harry Potter and the Sorcerer's Stone; *RIGHT: Jewelry with Celtic designs often enhanced McGonagall's neckline, as seen in* Harry Potter and the Chamber of Secrets.

The Sorting Hat

Professor McGonagall manages the Sorting Ceremony at Hogwarts when Harry Potter is sorted into Gryffindor in Harry Potter and the Sorcerer's Stone. During the Sorting Ceremony, the Sorting Hat is placed upon the head of each first-year student, and then sorts the student into one of four houses. Though neither human nor creature, the hat exhibits its own distinctive and imposing character.

The filmmaker's first attempt at bringing the Sorting Hat to cinematic life, in Harry Potter and the Sorcerer's Stone, was as a puppet. But as Judianna Makovsky explains, "It didn't look like a hat. It looked like a puppet." Director Chris Columbus asked Makovsky to fabricate a Hat, to which Makovsky responded, "Well, I can make a hat, but I can't make it talk." When the hat was brought to the set, it pleased the filmmakers but confused second unit director Robert Legato, who asked how it would talk. "And Chris looked at him and said, 'Well, she made the hat, you make it talk.'" The Hat was voiced by actor Leslie Phillips, whose distinctive sound benefitted from elocution lessons as a child in order to lose his original Cockney accent.

The hat Makovsky constructed wasn't actually used for the Sorting Ceremony. Instead, an apparatus that works in a way similar to motion capture technology was placed on the actors' heads and the talking hat was animated digitally. But the Sorting Hat was realized in full, out of suede, and lined with horsehair canvas for its place in Dumbledore's office in Harry Potter and the Chamber of Secrets and for the final battle of Hogwarts in Harry Potter and the Deathly Hallows – Part 2. Over the course of the films, seven hats were created, which start out in a cone form. Costume fabricator Steve Kill soaks the material in hot water for ten minutes to soften it, then "squashes it down into itself." This is left overnight above a heating unit, and the next day the hat is rigged with wire inside to keep its form. Each hat is then dyed, "broken down" to give it age, and printed lightly with Celtic symbols. As Kill admits, the wrinkles are different on each hat, but "of course, you never see them next to each other."

TOP: *The Sorting Hat;* ABOVE LEFT: *Costume fabricator Steve Kill works on one of several iterations of the Sorting Hat;*
ABOVE RIGHT: *Continuity shot on the Great Hall set, Harry Potter and the Sorcerer's Stone.*

Professor Sprout

Herbology Professor Pomona Sprout's wardrobe for *Harry Potter and the Chamber of Secrets* is as organic as her subject matter. Dressed in a palette of earth tones, leafy shapes are used as accents on her robes: greenery seems to grow from her cuffs and cape-like collar. The witch's hat she wears in the greenhouse is constructed in a burlap-style material, and "sprouts" leaves from the tip. As she works with plants such as Mandrakes and Venomous Tentacula leaves, she wears a pair of thick, beat-up gloves, bolstered with twine, and, of course, sports a large pair of ear muffs.

Sprout's outfit appeared more utilitarian in *Harry Potter and the Deathly Hallows – Part 2*. She wears a pair of thick blue overalls and a checkered shirt beneath her robe, which resembles a late eighteenth-century smock-coat. Smock-coats, featuring the characteristic pleats called "tubes," were used primarily by agricultural workers, as they provided both warmth and elasticity.

FIRST APPEARANCE:
Harry Potter and the Chamber of Secrets

ADDITIONAL APPEARANCE:
Harry Potter and the Deathly Hallows – Part 2

HOUSE:
Hufflepuff

OCCUPATION:
Herbology professor,
Head of Hufflepuff House

SPROUT'S WAND

The rough surface of Pomona Sprout's wand resembles the grainy, diveted wood of a tree branch. The prop modelers looked extensively for interestingly shaped or textured pieces of wood, whether precious hardwoods or not, and tried to fashion the wand to the wizard.

INSET: *Miriam Margoyles as Professor Pomona Sprout;* OPPOSITE TOP: *Concept art by Andrew Williamson of the Herbology greenhouse in* Harry Potter and the Chamber of Secrets; OPPOSITE BOTTOM: *The organically dressed Professor Sprout among the Mandrakes in* Chamber of Secrets; RIGHT: *Costume sketch by Mauricio Carneiro of Jany Termime's new design for Sprout's robe;* ABOVE: *The professor had a more manufactured look in* Harry Potter and the Deathly Hallows – Part 2.

PROFESSOR FLITWICK

In *Harry Potter and the Sorcerer's Stone* and *Harry Potter and the Chamber of Secrets*, Warwick Davis portrays Charms Professor Filius Flitwick as wizened, silver-bearded, bald, and academically gowned. The next time Davis portrays Flitwick on-screen, in *Harry Potter and the Prisoner of Azkaban*, the teacher is a mustachioed, black-haired younger man attired in a tailed tuxedo.

"The change between *Chamber of Secrets* and *Prisoner of Azkaban* is the question I get asked the most by fans," Davis declares. It came about when his character simply didn't make it into the script for *Harry Potter and the Prisoner of Azkaban*. Producer David Heyman called the actor to apologize and then asked if he was interested in playing another role—that of the Frog Choir conductor. Davis, director Alfonso Cuarón, and special creature effects designer Nick Dudman devised the formal, operatically themed look. When Davis returned to play Flitwick in *Harry Potter and the Goblet of Fire*, director Mike Newell wanted the look kept, and so in addition to Charms, Flitwick became what Davis calls the "professor of magical music."

The original Flitwick makeup took four hours; the new version took only two and a half. "And I think a lot of people on the set don't know what I *really* look like," Davis says with a laugh, "because I arrive a few hours before everyone else and go home later, after the makeup's removed." The younger Flitwick's makeup consists of a prosthetic forehead that wraps around to the back under a hair piece. Davis also wears fake ears, a fake nose, and false teeth. "I love the teeth, and want my own set so I can do toothpaste commercials," he teases.

The younger, fitter look inspired Davis to suggest a bit of business for *Harry Potter and the Goblet of Fire*. "At the end of the Yule Ball, my character introduces a rock band. So, stupidly, on a Friday evening, I said to Mike, 'Wouldn't it be funny if, after he introduces them, Flitwick dives off the stage and crowd-surfs?' We all had a laugh and I went home." On Monday, Davis suddenly found himself in consultation with stunt coordinator Greg Powell. It turns out Newell and Powell had gone to a club over the weekend, seen what Davis had mentioned, and decided to make it a reality. "And I said, 'Pardon?' But I didn't have the heart to tell them I was joking." So the stunt went off, with Flitwick being passed over the student's heads. "And at one point, if you look very closely," Davis advises, "you can actually see my false teeth fly out of my mouth and come back in again!"

Sc 106 Prof Flitwick.

FIRST APPEARANCE:
Harry Potter and the Sorcerer's Stone

ADDITIONAL APPEARANCES:
Harry Potter and the Chamber of Secrets
Harry Potter and the Prisoner of Azkaban
Harry Potter and the Goblet of Fire
Harry Potter and the Order of the Phoenix
Harry Potter and the Half-Blood Prince
Harry Potter and the Deathly Hallows – Part 2

HOUSE:
Ravenclaw

OCCUPATION:
Charms professor, Head of Ravenclaw House, Frog Choir conductor

FLITWICK'S WAND

Professor Flitwick's tapered wand has a design that flows seamlessly from the tip to the handle. The shape resembles a stylized streamlined arrow, with four "feathers" on the fletching end that come together near the darkened tip. In Flitwick's initial appearance as director of the Frog Choir in *Harry Potter and the Prisoner of Azkaban*, he wields a baton worthy of any wand. In *Harry Potter and the Goblet of Fire*, his baton was fashioned from a clear resin that matched the icicle-based decor of the room.

"Do you all have your feathers?"

Professor Flitwick, *Harry Potter and the Sorcerer's Stone*

INSET: *Warwick Davis as the first incarnation of Professor Filius Flitwick;* OPPOSITE BOTTOM AND RIGHT: *Flitwick's original robes showcased exotic fabrics, as seen in a continuity shot on the set of* Harry Potter and the Sorcerer's Stone, *a costume reference shot, and a scene from the same film;* RIGHT AND ABOVE: *Warwick Davis as Flitwick in* Harry Potter and the Goblet of Fire, *a look picked up from the choir master's suit from* Harry Potter and the Prisoner of Azkaban *as seen in Jany Temime's design, sketched by Mauricio Carneiro.*

PROFESSOR TRELAWNEY

When asked once to sum up her character, Divination Professor Sybill Trelawney, in one sentence, Emma Thompson simply stated, "Mad as a bucket of snakes." Jany Temime agreed with the actress that Trelawney was mad "but she has a reason to be mad. She has trouble coping with her life, her job. We could go far in doing something completely absurd and ridiculous because the actor put a sensibility behind it." Thompson felt that Trelawney was someone who hadn't looked in a mirror for a long time, who, in fact, "just couldn't see anything at all," she says. "So I thought if she hasn't looked at herself, if she can't see herself, then she must look all sorts of undone. Buttons missing, clothes a bit raggedy." The actress illustrated her thoughts about Trelawney's look and sent them to director Alfonso Cuarón, who passed them to Temime. Temime felt Thompson's design was "pretty unbeatable." She was clearly influenced by the pervading theme of sight—whether of one's self or of the future—and Temime embellished many of Trelawney's outfits with a form of Indian embroidery called shisha. Shisha embroidery employs mirrors or other reflective material; these are shaped in ovals and circles that create the illusion of Trelawney being covered in eyes.

INSET: *Emma Thompson as Professor Sybill Trelawney;* BOTTOM: *Initial costume designs for Trelawney by Jany Temime included turbans topping the multiple layers of clothing.*

FIRST APPEARANCE:
Harry Potter and the Prisoner of Azkaban

ADDITIONAL APPEARANCES:
Harry Potter and the Order of the Phoenix
Harry Potter and the Deathly Hallows – Part 2

HOUSE:
Ravenclaw

OCCUPATION:
Divination professor

ADDITIONAL SKILL SET:
Seer

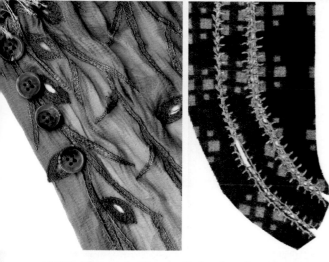

Thompson worked with the hair and makeup department to generate Trelawney's wild do. "I had this notion of her having hair that just kind of exploded at the top of her head and clearly had not been brushed in a long, long time. Probably has had squirrels nesting in it at some point," Thompson teases. "One doesn't know what would be found if you went too far into it." Trelawney's huge coke-bottle eyeglasses added the final right touch. "I just knew she had to have these huge eyes," Thompson explains. "The glasses made my eyes enormous, but, of course, they were difficult to see through. So as she's entering the classroom and talking about having 'the sight,' she walks into a table. Her entrance is one of the oldest and cheapest gags in the book, and I take full responsibility for it."

ABOVE: *Shisha embroidery details show how the mirrored pieces added additional texture to Trelawney's robes and shawls;* BELOW: *Costume development art sketched by Mauricio Carneiro for* Harry Potter and the Deathly Hallows – Part 2 *and* Harry Potter and the Order of the Pheonix; RIGHT: *A publicity photo for* Harry Potter and the Order of the Pheonix.

TRELAWNEY'S WAND

Sybill Trelawney's wand, rendered in a single length of wood, has a swirl spiraling around the shaft, and a flattened handle. Several of the astronomical symbols on the handle refer to minor planets and asteroids, including Ceres, Hebe, and Melpomene.

"Could you please predict something for me?"

Dolores Umbridge, *Harry Potter and the Order of the Phoenix*

Professor Snape

During a costume consultation between Alan Rickman and Judianna Makovsky, the actor who plays Professor Severus Snape had two firm requests—the sleeves should be tight, and there should be lots of buttons. "I wanted great care taken in every aspect of the character, both psychological and practical," Rickman explains. "The cut of the hair, the length of the dress robes, the makeup." Rickman considers that his costume is an important part of the very focused life that Snape has led. "You know that he lives a solitary kind of existence, you're not quite sure what the details of that are. He doesn't have much of a social life, and clearly, he's only got one set of clothes," he ends with a laugh. "The costume helped me to understand somebody who lives absolutely alone. Whereas the different costume designers made all sorts of changes through the films to the characters, my costume stayed exactly the same for all eight films. And it helped me, thinking that's the only thing hanging in his wardrobe."

Judianna Makovsky decided that while Dumbledore was very medieval, Snape would follow the Dickensian style. His severe gown is made from traditional academic fabric, ironed until it develops an unusual shine; it is actually a dark blue, which photographs black on film. Buttons run up to his neck, up his long sleeves, and even on his pants over his boots. Snape's robes showcase one very unique element. "We lengthened and split the train so that when he walks, you see these two little tongues that come out, like a snake's forked tongue," she explains. "So in a way, he literally slithers out of a room."

FIRST APPEARANCE:
Harry Potter and the Sorcerer's Stone

ADDITIONAL APPEARANCES:
Harry Potter and the Chamber of Secrets
Harry Potter and the Prisoner of Azkaban
Harry Potter and the Goblet of Fire
Harry Potter and the Order of the Phoenix
Harry Potter and the Half-Blood Prince
Harry Potter and the Deathly Hallows – Part 1
Harry Potter and the Deathly Hallows – Part 2

HOUSE:
Slytherin

OCCUPATION:
Potions Master, Defense of the Dark Arts professor (sixth year), Head of Slytherin House, Headmaster of Hogwarts (seventh year)

MEMBER OF:
Death Eaters, Order of the Phoenix

PATRONUS:
Doe

"Always."

Severus Snape, *Harry Potter and the Deathly Hallows – Part 2*

INSET: *Alan Rickman as Professor Severus Snape;* OPPOSITE: *A publicity photo for* Harry Potter and the Sorcerer's Stone; ABOVE: *Snape's first Potions class with Harry Potter in Sorcerer's Stone;* RIGHT: *Ron Weasley and Harry Potter receive a warning from Snape in* Harry Potter and the Goblet of Fire.

Jany Temime calls the design of Snape's outfit "a winner. He's a man who never explodes out of his clothes, so he must wear something extremely strict and precise." Rickman concurs. "He lives within very tight confines—physically as well as emotionally." He also offers a practical appreciation for his wardrobe. "Leavesden Studios didn't have the best heating system in the world, so I was more fortunate than others with my costume, which was always pretty warm."

Throughout the filming of the Harry Potter series it was rumored that author J.K. Rowling had told Alan Rickman Snape's deepest secret—that of his love for Harry's mother, Lily. For ten years, Rickman exhibited the same kind of steadfast loyalty as his character, never revealing to anyone what she had said. It wasn't until after the final film that he confirmed the rumor was true. Producer David Heyman, who knew that Rickman had been given key information, admits, "There were times when a director would tell Alan what to do in a scene and he would say, 'No, I can't do that.' Looking back, you can see there was always more going on there—a look, an expression, a sentiment—that hint at what is to come . . . the shadow he casts in these films is a huge one and the emotion he conveys is immeasurable."

SNAPE'S WAND

Severus Snape's slim wand is fashioned in a dark, ebony black, with an intricate, unique design that is doubled on both sides of the handle. The majority of wands used for filming were cast in resin or a urethane rubber; wood versions were used for close-ups. Actor Alan Rickman is one of the few actors who was able to keep one of the original wood wands he used on set.

OPPOSITE TOP LEFT: *Professors Snape and McGonagall inspect the cursed necklace in* Harry Potter and the Half-Blood Prince; *OPPOSITE BOTTOM LEFT: Snape's buttoned-up pants leg; OPPOSITE RIGHT: The professor's Edwardian suit never changed through the course of eight films; TOP AND ABOVE: Costume sketches for the Boggart-version of Snape wearing Neville Longbottom's grandmother's clothes in* Harry Potter and the Prisoner of Azkaban *(design by Jany Temime, sketches by Laurent Guinci) and the realized version from the film; LEFT: A closer look at the "forked tail" of Snape's robes designed by Judianna Makovsky for* Harry Potter and the Sorcerer's Stone.

PROFESSOR QUIRRELL

Harry Potter and the Sorcerer's Stone costume designer Judianna Makovsky's concept for all the Hogwarts professors was to evoke formal British school attire, which incorporates suits and ties under the teachers' robes. For Defense Against the Dark Arts Professor Quirrell's outfit, Makovsky was tasked to add a turban, which Quirrell, played by Ian Hart, wears to hide the fact that he is sharing his body with the disembodied form of Lord Voldemort. "The book was specific that he wore a turban," says Makovsky, "but I was concerned that the turban didn't look too exotic or out of place." She moved away from using Middle Eastern– or Indian-style turbans, which are traditionally closer to the head in back and raised to a more pointed form. Instead, Makovsky chose a design from the Renaissance, as the wrappings are larger and less constricting so it wouldn't seem obvious that Quirrell was hiding something. In order to downplay the character, who is purposely trying not to be conspicuous, she chose flat blacks and browns for his suits, which suggested a shy person and an impoverished status.

Actor Ian Hart received a funny shock when he went to research the character before meeting with the producers and casting director of Harry Potter and the Sorcerer's Stone. "I'd never read any of the books, so I went to a local bookshop," he explains, "and they gave me the second book, Harry Potter and the Chamber of Secrets." Professor Quirrell, of course, doesn't make it past the first book. "I was looking through it, thinking 'Where's my character? It can't be that big a part, as I can't find it!'"

PROFESSOR QUIRREL

WIZARD GOWN · LINING TO WIZARD GOWN · CAPE · TIE · JACKET · MRS. E W/COAT · TURBAN

FABRIC SWATCHES   02/02/2001

INSET: *Ian Hart as Professor Quirinus Quirrell*; ABOVE LEFT: *A close-up of Quirrell's plain-colored coat for Harry Potter and the Sorcerer's Stone*; ABOVE RIGHT: *Costume swatches on a reference sheet*; RIGHT: *The Renaissance-inspired turban worn by Quirrell hides a dark secret*; OPPOSITE TOP LEFT: *The turban in the costume shop*; OPPOSITE TOP RIGHT: *A digital rendition of Voldemort's face positioned on the back of Quirrell's head*; OPPOSITE BOTTOM: *An early depiction of the snakelike face of Lord Voldemort by visual artist Paul Catling.*

"Who would suspect p-p-p-poor st-t-t-stuttering Professor Quirrell?"

Professor Quirrell, *Harry Potter and the Sorcerer's Stone*

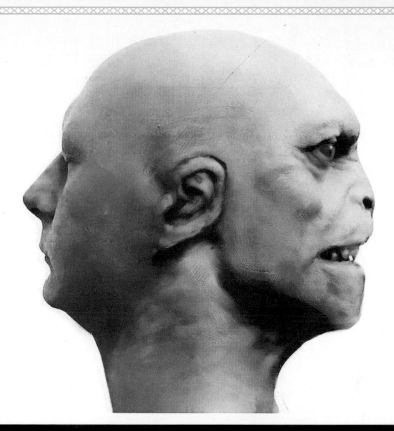

PROFESSOR LOCKHART

Actor Kenneth Branagh happily offers an analysis of the character he plays in *Harry Potter and the Chamber of Secrets*, Professor Gilderoy Lockhart. "He's wonderfully cowardly, fantastically unreliable, totally out for number one, ruthlessly ambitious, and desperate to be loved. Whatever you've done, he can do better. He lives for trumping people. It's not possible for him to be in a room and be in second place.

"He is also a great showman. An entrance into a classroom is another performance. He has one eye on the audience; he has one eye on the mirror. He's just a wonderfully puffed up character and these are all qualities that are good fun to play."

Lockhart's attention to how he appears is reflected in his wardrobe, of course. For that, "We looked at reference of old movie actors and cinema idols from the twenties through to the fifties," says *Harry Potter and the Chamber of Secrets* associate costume designer Michael O'Connor. "Anyone who's read the book knows that Gilderoy is a very vain man," adds *Chamber of Secrets* costume designer Lindy Hemming, "and has created this fabulous persona for himself. He wants to create a large and glorious impression, and sweeps about in gowns that are colorful." However, director Chris Columbus had a strong view that there were to be no strong or bright colors used for the costumes that would distract from the actor's performance. "Lockhart was known for wearing lilac and pink and powder blue and these pastels weren't within the color scheme of the Harry Potter films," explains Hemming. Multiple screen tests allowed the filmmakers to find grayish blues, golden mustards, and brownish pinks that would fit the overall palette of the film but still make Lockhart look brighter than the characters around him. He wore lush-looking fabrics—gold-embroidered velvets, silk damasks, brocades, and moirés—and sported an extensive collection of matching capes and cravats. Branagh's makeup included a set of perfect, sparkling false teeth, and wigs that needed to look like wigs, as Lockhart is seen packing away a hairpiece in his attempt to flee Hogwarts. He was also outfitted in an array of exotic outfits to create the book covers for his many best-selling books and framed photos strewn about his classroom.

INSET: *Kenneth Branagh as Professor Gilderoy Lockhart;* RIGHT: *A collection of books chronicles a series of adventures Lockhart never actualy had, designed by Miraphona Mina and Eduardo Lima for* Harry Potter and the Chamber of Secrets; FAR RIGHT: *The professor in his classroom;* OPPOSITE TOP LEFT AND CENTER: *Costume reference photos;* OPPOSITE CENTER: *Lockhart attempts the* Brachium Amendo *spell on Harry Potter's arm;* OPPOSITE BOTTOM LEFT: *A continuity sheet explains the proper way to tie Lockhart's cravat;* OPPOSITE BOTTOM RIGHT: *Lockhart's duelling costume.*

COSTUME CONTINUITY REPORT

CHARACTER:	ACTOR:
GILDEROY LOCKHART	KENNETH BRANAGH

COSTUME NUMBER: 2

SCENES:	STORY DAY:
42 A + B	7

LOCATION:
INT: LOCKHARTS CLASSROOM

DESCRIPTION:
ROBE: GOLD SLEEVELES WITH FLORAL FACINGS, TURNED BACK WHILST SEATED
COAT: 3/4 FROCK COAT, NO BUTTONS
WAISTCOAT: GOLD FLORAL PATTERN SILK BROCADE, ALL BUTTONS FASTENED REVERS TURNED BACK (NOT FLAT) OUTSIDE OF COAT AND ROBE
TROUSERS: MUSTARD CROSS WEAVE WORN WITH BRACES

SHIRT: IVORY, FIXED CHARGE COLLAR, TWO TOP BUTTONS FASTENED CUFFS WITH GOLD MONOGRAMMED LINKS AS BELOW
CRAVAT: IVORY SILK BROCADE WITH LARGE BOW AS BELOW

BOOTS: LIGHT BROWN ELASTIC SIDED, RUBBERISED SOLE

NOTES:

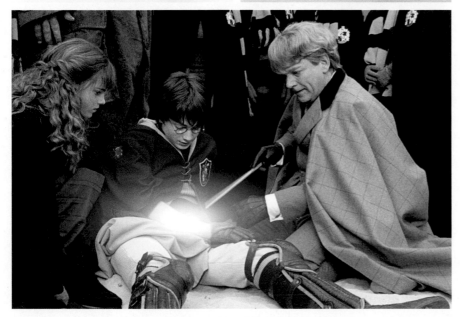

LOCKHART'S WAND

Gilderoy Lockhart's wand may appear simple, as do most of the wands for the first two films, but was finished with a lily design at the top. In a reverse from many of the wands, the shaft was constructed from a light wood and the handle was black. Actor Kenneth Branagh (Lockhart) gave great consideration to his wand moves for his duel with Severus Snape in *Harry Potter and the Chamber of Secrets*. "If you are down the other end of the platform from Alan Rickman," says Branagh, "and he's got a wand, you've got to be very good to get noticed down at your end!"

"Let me introduce you to your new Defense Against the Dark Arts teacher. Me!"

Gilderoy Lockhart, *Harry Potter and the Chamber of Secrets*

Professor Lupin

As David Thewlis began filming his role as Defense Against Dark Arts Professor Remus Lupin for *Harry Potter and the Prisoner of Azkaban*, he had the impression that "the part was just a one-off," as Lupin does not appear in the fourth book, *Harry Potter and the Goblet of Fire*. But then he heard rumors that Lupin would be coming back. When *Harry Potter and the Order of the Phoenix* was published halfway through the third film's production, Thewlis stood in line among the young witch-and-wizard attired fans at his local bookstore's midnight party. "I picked up a copy, and while standing in line started leafing through to see if Lupin was mentioned. And sure enough, I saw he was, quite early on." Thewlis was delighted that he would be able to return for *Harry Potter and the Order of the Phoenix*, and then went to the end of the book to see if his character made it all the way through, as there were rumors that one major character did not. "I saw that Lupin made it, but accidentally caught sight of Sirius Black being talked about in the past tense." As fate would have it, Thewlis bumped into his neighbor Gary Oldman the next morning, who also had a copy of the book but hadn't sneaked at look at the ending. "So, Gary asks if I'd seen the book, and I was like, yeah, oh yeah, yeah. And he says, 'We've got a lot of work to do, mate.' Oh yeah, yeah, okay. I didn't have the heart to tell him he wasn't going to make it all the way through."

In *Harry Potter and the Prisoner of Azkaban*, it's discovered that Lupin is a werewolf, an iconic "movie monster" that Thewlis and director Alfonso Cuarón were determined to give a fresh approach. Cuarón saw Lupin as "your favorite uncle who is hiding a horrible disease. Instead of being healthy and powerful, he's sick. It's tragic, not scary." Thewlis agreed, and opted that he only had to address the transformation when Lupin actually

FIRST APPEARANCE:
Harry Potter and the Prisoner of Azkaban

ADDITIONAL APPEARANCES:
Harry Potter and the Order of the Phoenix
Harry Potter and the Half-Blood Prince
Harry Potter and the Deathly Hallows – Part 1
Harry Potter and the Deathly Hallows – Part 2

HOUSE:
Gryffindor

OCCUPATION:
Defense Against the Dark Arts professor
(third year)

MEMBER OF:
Order of the Phoenix

ADDITIONAL INFORMATION:
Werewolf (Moony)

INSET: *David Thewlis as Professor Remus Lupin;* ABOVE: *Lupin with the Marauder's Map;* RIGHT: *Development artwork of a werewolf by Wayne Barlowe;* OPPOSITE, CLOCKWISE FROM TOP: *Harry Potter accompanied by Hedwig (Gizmo) spends time with Lupin; sketches by Mauricio Carneiro and fabric swatches for Lupin's simple suit; a publicity photo—all for Harry Potter and the Prisoner of Azkaban.*

"I've looked worse, believe me."

Remus Lupin, *Harry Potter and the Prisoner of Azkaban*

FINAL STAGE 3 COSTUME 9.
HARRY POTTER
& THE PRISONER OF AZKABAN
COSTUME CONTINUITY

CHARACTER	PROF LUPIN	ACTOR:	DAVID THEWLIS

FINAL STAGE ③

Sc 117 PT
N 13
LUPIN

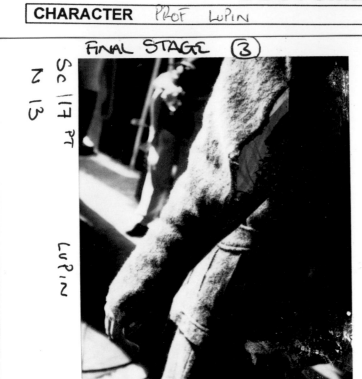

FINAL STAGE ③

SC 117 PT   LUPIN

N 13

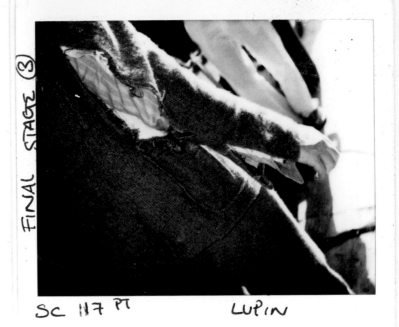

SCENE: 117	STORY D/N: 13	SCENE:	STORY D/N:

FINAL STAGE ③

SC 117   LUPIN

N 13

STAGE ② BACK RIP.

Sc 117 PT
N 13

LUPIN.

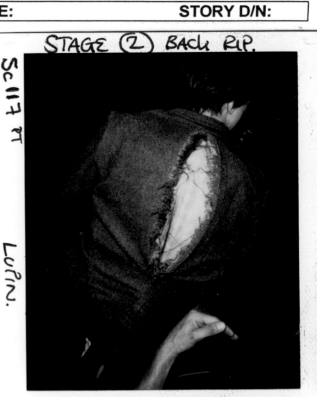

SCENE:	STORY D/N:	SCENE:	STORY D/N:

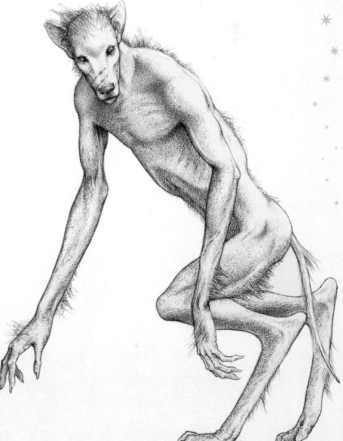

transformed. Otherwise, he says, "Lupin is that favorite teacher who is a little more social and friendly than would normally be the case." Thewlis was inspired by several of his former teachers as well as beloved cinematic professors such as in *Good-bye, Mr. Chips*.

Remus Lupin's illness has taken a toll on him in many ways, one being the state of his wardrobe. "It is written that Lupin's clothes are of poor quality and shabby," says Jany Temime. "So his suit and academy gown are drab and a bit threadbare. They're not like any of the other teachers." Lupin is still a very "tweedy professor," she continues. Regardless of the condition, Lupin's outfits are an example of her philosophy toward dressing the wizarding world. "In all their clothes," she explains, "we want what I think of as traditional construction to them. Lupin was given long, pointed sleeves, and on his jacket, the collar has a point on the back. His pockets have points on them as well. He is a typical English wizard."

LUPIN'S WAND

Remus Lupin's wand was crafted from olivewood, and its design "was quite gentle," describes Pierre Bohanna. "It's really the closest to a conductor's baton in its shape." The prop makers strove to give each wand a sense of timelessness. "They should look period, or at least look well used," adds Bohanna. "It should be difficult to judge how old the wands are." Actor David Thewlis (Lupin) hoped to take his wand home as a souvenir, but noted how careful the crew was to store the wands properly and safely after each scene. "It would have been like trying to take a nugget of gold out of a bank," he laughs.

OPPOSITE: *Continuity shots of the rips and tears of Lupin's clothing taken during his transformation to a werewolf;* THIS PAGE: *Visual development artwork of Lupin in his werewolf form by Wayne Barlowe.*

PROFESSOR MOODY

Alastor Moody's teaching style is a one-eighty from previous Defense Against the Dark Arts teachers. Moody is more about "tough love," says actor Brendan Gleeson. "He wants them to face the fact that evil exists; they'd better know what they're getting themselves into." But Moody's on their side, he avers, which is apparent in his performances in *Harry Potter and the Order of the Phoenix* and *Harry Potter and the Deathly Hallows – Part 1*.

"I think he's rather comforting to have around once we learn he was brought in to protect Harry." Gleeson does make the most of the ex-Auror's formidable personality. "Moody is a gunslinger with a wand. He's obviously suffered terrible trauma. This guy has gone past a sell-by date in the sense that he was out there at the cutting edge. And so he's become quite paranoid now, but that doesn't mean that everybody isn't out to get him, because they are!"

Jany Temime agrees with Gleeson's gunslinger analogy. "My inspiration was Spaghetti Westerns," she says. "Instead of a horse, the man rides into the sunset on his broomstick. And the man sleeps in his coat, he *lives* in his coat; all of his possessions are in that coat." "That coat" was inspired by a 1940s war coat, replicated in dark khaki and made to appear as if it was just as old. Breakdown artist Tim Shanahan explains that the process begins with blowtorches. "Any fiber on a coat has a fuzz to it that goes flat and shiny as it is gradually worn away, whether it's stitching or the entire coat itself. We use blowtorches to lightly burn off the tops of the fibers." Bleach is applied to lighten certain areas, or tar and paints are added to create stains. The coat is sanded and then stained again. The material is ripped and frayed with knives and scruffers—the name of a wire brush invented just for this task. Varnish flattens the shine of buttons, buckles, and zippers, which are also sanded down. Pockets are wetted and weighted down throughout this process, to get them to be baggy and saggy. This process is done to not only the actor's coat, but to their stunt doubles', and made in multiple versions due to wear and tear during filming. It took about eighty hours to create just one coat for Mad-Eye Moody, and seven coats were needed for the actor and his stunt doubles.

FIRST APPEARANCE:
Harry Potter and the Goblet of Fire

ADDITIONAL APPEARANCES:
Harry Potter and the Order of the Phoenix
Harry Potter and the Deathly Hallows – Part 1

OCCUPATION:
Ex-Auror, Defense Against the Dark Arts professor (fourth year)

MEMBER OF:
Order of the Phoenix

INSET: *Brendan Gleeson as Professor Alastor "Mad-Eye" Moody;* LEFT: *Close-up of the small bottle in Moody's coat pocket that holds Polyjuice Potion from* Harry Potter and the Deathly Hallows – Part 1; ABOVE: *Costume sketches by Mauricio Carneiro;* OPPOSITE: *Gleeson as Bartemius Crouch Jr. as Professor Mad-Eye Moody in "that coat" in a publicity shot for* Harry Potter and the Goblet of Fire.

Moody's signature feature—his "mad-eye"—is housed in a silicone prosthetic over which is strapped a brass "porthole"-shaped framework. The initial idea was to composite the eye digitally onto the actor's face. "We really fought against that," says Nick Dudman, "because we wanted it to be something Brendan Gleeson could work with even though he's not actually operating the eye." The challenge was to attach the eye in such a way that it didn't *look* attached. "We came up with the logic that he'd had to have had a massive injury where he'd lost his eye," says Dudman, "and so there is a build-up of scarring over that side of his face. And then Chris Barton, my animatronic designer, came up with the idea of placing a shell over the actor's eye that has a very small magnet—it's less than three millimeters thick—right behind the pupil of the mechanical eye that moves around via radio servers." If the magnet eye was pulled around too far, it would hit the side of its holder, breaking the magnetic link, and pop off. "And occasionally the eye line didn't quite match between the actor's, so they shifted it into place in post-production," admits Dudman, "but it was a nice, simple, practical answer."

Built up in several pieces, the prosthetic has channels that run through it to hide wires attached to the radio-controlled eye. Covering over the embedded wires are straps that also serve to secure it. The makeup and hair department then applies a wig over the prosthetic. "We fashioned the wig in panels that fit over all the mechanics," says Eithne Fennell. "We needed to create separate sections of hair because if anything went wrong with the eye, a panel could flap open so they could fix it and then we would put it back on again."

The Mad-Eye Moody seen in *Harry Potter and the Goblet of Fire* is actually a 'Polyjuice-Potioned' Bartemius Crouch Jr. "Moody is a character who is played by one actor," explains director Mike Newell, "who contains another actor inside him." Crouch Jr. is played by David Tennant, who describes being cast in a Harry Potter movie like "being called up to play for the England football squad—you don't necessarily expect it, but when it comes, it's the kind of honor you just can't turn down." Although a small part in the film, Tennant's performance is memorable, not the least for the deranged Death Eater's snakelike tongue-flick tic. "We needed something that would attach to both characters," explains Newell. Given this directive, Tennant improvised the quirk, which Brendan Gleeson then added to his portrayal.

> *"Ex-Auror, Ministry malcontent, and your new Defense Against the Dark Arts teacher. I'm here because Dumbledore asked me. End of story, goodbye, the end!"*
>
> Professor Moody, *Harry Potter and the Goblet of Fire*

MOODY'S WAND

Alastor Moody actually had four wands that he used, including one specifically designed to repair his silver leg in *Harry Potter and the Goblet of Fire*. "I asked if it could look like a replica of a spire in Dublin," says actor Brendan Gleeson. "It was used only once, but if I could have one, that would be the one I always cast my eye on, so to speak." Moody's main wand sported a round end that resembled the handle of his walking stick, and was banded in silver and bronze. The wand is shorter than most, seemingly having seen a lot of action.

OPPOSITE TOP LEFT: *Unit photography from* Harry Potter and the Goblet of Fire. OPPOSITE TOP RIGHT: *Early artwork of Mad-Eye by Wayne Barlowe;* OPPOSITE BOTTOM RIGHT: *A costume sketch by Mauricio Carneiro;* LEFT: *Moody's prosthetic leg as fashioned by Adam Brockbank;* TOP: *Concept art by Adam Brockbank.*

PROFESSOR UMBRIDGE

After *Harry Potter and the Order of the Phoenix*, the fifth Harry Potter book, was published, a friend of Imelda Staunton's phoned her to suggest there was a part in it Staunton should play. "So I read it again," recalls Staunton, "and the description was 'Short, fat, ugly, toad-like woman.' Oh, thanks for that!" But Staunton recognized that Dolores Umbridge is "just a delicious baddie. And I wouldn't have to spend too much time hanging from a crane." Staunton wondered initially if Umbridge would look as described in the book. "Will she be literally toad-like, and would I have prosthetics?" No prosthetics are used, but Staunton did ask for something extra to be added to the character's look. "She wanted to give her a big bottom," says Jany Temime. "She's actually a very thin woman." Padding was added front and back that inspired Staunton to create a distinctive walk, "like a duck," laughs Temime. Umbridge's physicality is stiff, rehearsed, almost robotic, at odds with the impression she's trying to create of being nice. "And she's not a real teacher," Temime explains. "She doesn't want to look like a teacher. She wants to look like a woman who is sent from the Ministry." Temime created a silhouette that is prim and elegant, with peculiar touches of girlishness. "I wanted her costumes to appear serious, but always with one detail that was just a bit too much. So maybe the bow is too big or the combination of fabrics is crude. Imelda had a strong opinion about what she wanted," she concludes, "but luckily I had the same opinion."

Umbridge's ensembles are accessorized with brooches, pins, and rings—all bearing an image of a cat, like those on the walls of her office. The character is written as having a decidedly pink theme to her wardrobe—even her wizard robes are pink—and Temime appreciated how Rowling had put one of her hardest-edged characters in a very soft

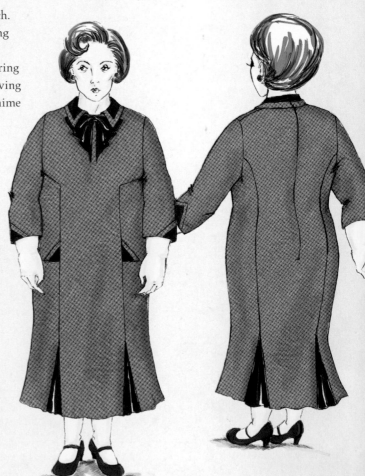

INSET: *Imelda Staunton as Professor Dolores Umbridge;* RIGHT AND OPPOSITE TOP LEFT: *Costume designs by Jany Temime show not only the outfit but a progression of ever-darkening pinks. Sketches by Mauricio Carneiro;* OPPOSITE LEFT: *A simple outfit with girlish flourishes and ubiquitous cat jewelry as worn by Imelda Staunton in a publicity photo for* Harry Potter and the Order of the Phoenix; OPPOSITE TOP RIGHT: *Fabric swatches;* OPPOSITE CENTER AND BOTTOM RIGHT: *More feline jewelry and a pair of pink pumps.*

FIRST APPEARANCE:
Harry Potter and the Order of the Phoenix

ADDITIONAL APPEARANCE:
Harry Potter and the Deathly Hallows – Part 1

OCCUPATION:
Senior Undersecretary to the Minister for Magic, Defense Against the Dark Arts professor (fifth year), Hogwarts High Inquisitor and Headmistress, Head of Hogwarts Inquisitorial Squad and Ministry of Magic's Muggle-Born Registration Commission

PATRONUS:
Cat

color. She seized the opportunity to use the contradiction to the character's advantage. Umbridge is initially attired in mild pink dresses that become darker and darker until her last outfit, which is fashioned in an almost electric fuchsia Temime deemed "acidic and aggressive." To stress the incongruity even more, fabrics with soft textures were used—handwoven tweeds, velours, velvets, and angora from Paris. Staunton and Temime were again in complete agreement about this. "I wanted her to appear soft," says Staunton, "which I discussed with Jany. I didn't want any hard edges; I thought it was quite important for her to have a softness and a warmth to her look. What's more frightening than a little round woolly person who turns out to be not very nice? She's so dedicated to helping these children to see the light. Or to see the pink, I think."

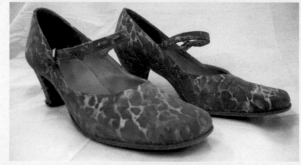

UMBRIDGE'S WAND

Not surprisingly, Dolores Umbridge's wand has a bit of pink in it. The wand as a whole is designed with a series of very ornate turns, and a very pointed end, but within the middle is a round, deep pink jewel. The wand was created in purple mahogany wood but cast in a clear color of resin before staining it.

Professor Slughorn

By the time Jim Broadbent joined the Harry Potter films as Potions Professor Horace Slughorn, he had already played a rich diversity of roles in more than one hundred films. *Harry Potter and the Half-Blood Prince* offered him a new acting challenge. "When we first meet my character," he explains, "I am disguised as an armchair." Did Broadbent have anything in his long career he could draw upon? "I did a voice-over of a lavatory seat once. But this is my first real chair." Jany Temime sourced the lilac-colored material that transforms from upholstery into pajamas, but this was just the first piece of Slughorn's extensive wardrobe.

Temime believes that Slughorn isn't the clotheshorse that Dumbledore is, but is "somebody who just has the right outfit for the right occasion." She feels that he has been holding on to his clothes for twenty-five years or so, and that though they have remained fashionable, they are a bit worn and shabby. "He just keeps wearing them, and perhaps that is to recapture his glory," she muses. "Once upon a time these clothes were quite beautiful, but now they're so used, buttons are hanging off, his shoes are damaged, the fabric has been mended again and again." We are offered a chance to see the clothes in their original condition, when a memory of his time teaching Tom Riddle is seen through the Pensieve. Jim Broadbent was padded to give him girth and age, which was removed for his "younger" scenes.

FIRST APPEARANCE:
Harry Potter and the Half-Blood Prince

ADDITIONAL APPEARANCE:
Harry Potter and the Deathly Hallows – Part 2

HOUSE:
Slytherin

OCCUPATION:
Potions Master

INSET: *Jim Broadbent as Professor Horace Slughorn;* LEFT AND OPPOSITE CENTER AND RIGHT: *Slughorn's extensive wardrobe as seen in sketches for Harry Potter and the Half-Blood Prince;* ABOVE: *In a flashback, Slughorn's clothes are in much better shape;* OPPOSITE LEFT: *Slughorn's "Oxbridge" style robes;* OPPOSITE RIGHT: *Fabric swatches.*

SLUGHORN.

Quality	
Width	130cm.
Metres	
Shade	Col.5 VG TIEPOLO
T&G (Chelsea)	£60.90/m.

Quality	WOOL CHECK
Width	150
Metres	25 m.
Shade	
'EMREE' £51/m.	
Quality	SILK MOIRÉ OFF-WHITE.
Width	112 cm.
Metres	23.2 m.
Shade	
Broadwick silk £35/m.	
Quality	BROWN BROCADE.
Width	130
Metres	
Shade	
Broadwick silk.	
Quality	
Width	140.
Metres	
Shade	
Broadwick silk	
Quality	VELVET CROCO PRINT
Width	
Metres	12.80
Shade	
Berwick St cloth shop.	
Quality	WOOL. CHECK.
Width	150
Metres	8 m.
Shade	
CLOTH HOUSE. (98).	

USED 3... FABRIC

1 M/ Gostin 6-10

"But that's life, I suppose!

You—you go along and

then suddenly . . . poof."

Professor Slughorn, *Harry Potter and the Half-Blood Prince*

Slughorn's clothes reflect classic English tailoring—three-piece suits, tweeds, and bowties in rusts, browns, and beiges—"but always with a twist. He wears fabric that's a little bit louder, a print that stands out a bit too much." Temime thought of him as "an eccentric dandy," and wanted to show that he enjoys the finer things in life, utilizing velours, damasks, and silks. She gave him Oxbridge-style professor's robes, and a tasseled mortarboard hat. Calling something Oxbridge, a word blending the two universities Oxford and Cambridge, suggests a superior intellectual or social status, something she thinks Slughorn endeavors to convey. "He's proud of being an academic," she says, "and it was important to show that." Slughorn also wears an Inverness-style brown-checked cape and a white coat collared and cuffed in fur "from an animal only wizards know."

Once Slughorn's wardrobe was assembled, Tim Shanahan's breakdown crew's work began. Slughorn's woolen suits were aged by burning fibers off to thin out areas that logically have the most wear, around the shoulders, cuffs, and pockets. Bright colors were washed out, and a special powder solution was used to give it the appearance of an accumulation of dust that just can't be washed out. How far do outfits get broken down? "When we see through the lining, we stop," says Temime.

ABOVE: *Professor Slughorn hosts a party for potential "Slug Club" members in* Harry Potter and the Half-Blood Prince; *LEFT AND OPPOSITE TOP: More costume sketches by Mauricio Carneiro; RIGHT: Detail of Slughorn's robe made of the same material as a chair; OPPOSITE BOTTOM RIGHT: The Potions professor tries to snip off some* Venomous Tentacula *leaves before being interrupted by Harry Potter.*

SLUGHORN'S WAND

Concept artists Adam Brockbank designed Horace Slughorn's wand clearly with the professor's name in mind. "It's like a slug, really," Brockbank explains, "so there are two curves in its length to the hilt, and then at the end there's this sort of lump with the two eyes of a snail, done in an amber-looking material." The handle is gun-metal silver, and the shaft has what Brockbank calls a "slug trail design that's silver-inlaid into the wood." The thick casting, with its large amount of metal inlay work, was one of the heaviest wands created for the films.

THE GHOSTS OF HOGWARTS

ABOVE: *Visual development artwork by Adam Brockbank of the "Deathday" party from* Harry Potter and the Chamber of Secrets *book that didn't make it into the film;* OPPOSITE TOP: *Nearly Headless Nick (John Cleese) demonstrates why he is "nearly headless";* OPPOSITE BOTTOM: *Continuity shots for* Chamber of Secrets.

FIRST APPEARANCE:
Harry Potter and the Sorcerer's Stone

ADDITIONAL APPEARANCES:
Harry Potter and the Chamber of Secrets
Harry Potter and the Order of the Phoenix
(deleted from film)

HOUSE:
Gryffindor

OCCUPATION:
Ghost

SIR NICHOLAS DE MIMSY-PORPINGTON, AKA NEARLY HEADLESS NICK

Judianna Makovsky was glad that the filming of the ghosts of Hogwarts for *Harry Potter and the Sorcerer's Stone* wasn't scheduled until near the very end of the movie. "It took us about nine months to figure out how to do them," she recalls. "They needed to be unusual, and they also needed to work for Robert Legato," the visual effects supervisor for *Harry Potter and the Sorcerer's Stone*. "Trying to find the right material that would work was a very long process." Makovsky alludes to several historical eras for the ghosts of Hogwarts: late Renaissance for the Grey Lady, Baroque/Rococo for the Bloody Baron, and generic monk for the Fat Friar. Sir Nicholas de Mimsy-Porpington, played by actor John Cleese, straddles the border between Elizabethan- and Jacobean-era clothing, wearing a doublet, breeches, and a thin ruff that encircles the "nearly headlessness" of the character. "I don't think I've ever laughed as much during a costume fitting," Makovsky states. "And John Cleese let me go to town. He was willing to wear it all, including some ridiculous pumpkin hose." Makovsky eventually found a mesh fabric for all the ghosts that had copper wire embedded in it so it was moldable, and would keep its shape. "I didn't want them to look sheer, like your traditional ghosts with chiffon waving all over the place. We've seen that before. I wanted it to be real clothes from a real period." This worked for Robert Legato, who also found working with John Cleese "a riot. He was only with my team for one day, so we worked hard to get all our jokes right with him." Legato acknowledges that ghosts have been seen on-screen before, "about a million times. So the challenge is how do you shoot a ghost these days and make it better than earlier ones?" In post-production, the ghosts were given a digital glow and trails of ghostly matter.

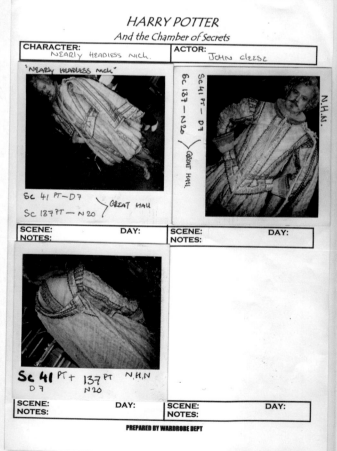

MOANING MYRTLE

Moaning Myrtle, a dead student who haunts the girls' bathroom in *Harry Potter and the Chamber of Secrets* and visits Harry Potter in the Prefects' bathroom in *Harry Potter and the Goblet of Fire*, is played by the distinctively voiced actress Shirley Henderson, who describes Myrtle's sound as "wounded. I did a lot of crying during the scenes and that aided that kind of gurgly quality I was trying to produce—as if she was choking on water all the time." Myrtle's school robes harken back to a time fifty years before present day events, made in a rough material with smocking near the collar. Any color in her outfit has been desaturated to gray. Henderson was strapped into a harness and flown in front of a green screen to create Myrtle's twists and turns. The filmed Myrtle was then rendered in a digital version. "She dives in and out of toilets, and bursts out of the plumbing system," says Emma Norton, visual effects producer. "Something that obviously had to be done in CGI!"

FIRST APPEARANCE:
Harry Potter and the Chamber of Secrets

ADDITIONAL APPEARANCE:
Harry Potter and the Goblet of Fire

HOUSE:
Ravenclaw

OCCUPATION:
Ghost

LEFT: *Shirley Henderson as Moaning Myrtle in a publicity photo for* Harry Potter and the Chamber of Secrets; TOP: *Artwork by Andrew Williamson of Moaning Myrtle hovering above Ron, Harry, and Professor Lockhart as the Chamber of Secrets is opened—not quite how it happened in the film;* OPPOSITE: *Actor Rik Mayall was cast as the mischievous Peeves in* Harry Potter and the Sorcerer's Stone, *but the ghost never made it past development artwork by Paul Catling.*

PEEVES

As happens regrettably when transferring a book to its filmed version, some characters don't make it into the final version. Peeves, a mischievous poltergeist that haunts Hogwarts' halls, was to be played by actor Rik Mayall in *Harry Potter and the Sorcerer's Stone*, but beyond costume sketches, the impish ghost did not manifest on-screen.

"If you die down there, you're welcome to share my toilet."

Moaning Myrtle, *Harry Potter and the Chamber of Secrets*

HELENA RAVENCLAW, AKA THE GREY LADY

The Grey Lady, originally played by Nina Young, is introduced along with the other Hogwarts ghosts at the opening feast in *Harry Potter and the Sorcerer's Stone*; in *Harry Potter and the Chamber of Secrets*, she also appears in a deleted scene. The true identity of Hogwarts' Grey Lady is finally revealed in *Harry Potter and the Deathly Hallows – Part 2* to be Helena Ravenclaw, daughter of the House's founder. Actress Kelly Macdonald, who at one time had been considered to play Tonks, landed the part, which was the last major role to be cast in the Harry Potter film series. Jany Temime chose a simpler, sleeker design than the original Grey Lady that is more medieval in style. The fitted dress has an embroidered undergown and laced overgown, both with long, draping sleeves.

FIRST APPEARANCE:
Harry Potter and the Sorcerer's Stone

ADDITIONAL APPEARANCES:
Harry Potter and the Chamber of Secrets
Harry Potter and the Deathly Hallows – Part 2

HOUSE:
Ravenclaw

OCCUPATION:
Ghost

"If you have to ask, you'll never know. If you know, you need only ask . . ."

Helena Ravenclaw, *Harry Potter and the Deathly Hallows – Part 2*

FAR LEFT: *Rowena Ravenclaw, the head of Ravenclaw House, was intended to appear in* Harry Potter and the Deathly Hallows – Part 2, *but her scenes were cut from the film;* LEFT AND ABOVE: *Helena Ravenclaw's costume had a simple medieval silhouette in* Deathly Hallows – Part 2. *Designs by Jany Temime and sketches by Mauricio Carneiro;* OPPOSITE: *Nina Young poses as the first Elizabethan-style Grey Lady, as seen in* Harry Potter and the Sorcerer's Stone.

Chapter 3

STUDENT ROBES & QUIDDITCH SPORTSWEAR

STUDENT ROBES

To *Harry Potter and the Sorcerer's Stone* costume designer Judianna Makovsky, students attending a "traditional English school," which Hogwarts is in its own way, meant creating a school uniform. "But J.K. Rowling said that the kids did not wear uniforms. In fact, it was considered more interesting to *not* have uniforms. It was rooted in the English school system, but it was also fantasy." Makovsky still felt strongly in a unified look. "So we tested Harry (Daniel Radcliffe) in modern clothes, and then tested him in the uniform." The filmmakers agreed with Makovsky that the uniforms worked better visually. And with costumes needed in multiples versions for the four hundred children playing Hogwarts students, "I have to say it saved our lives, because imagine trying to dress that many children in individuals outfits!"

The first Hogwarts uniforms consisted of gray flannel trousers for the boys and gray flannel pleated skirts for the girls, white shirts for both. "Sometimes they wore a sweater vest, sometimes they had a sweater with their house colors on it, and each had a house tie." The first years started out with a black tie, but this was soon exchanged for one with the Hogwarts symbol on it. The students' robes were based on traditional academic gowns, "with a small twist of sorts to give them wizard sleeves." The robes were so comfortable that Daniel Radcliffe described them as feeling like pajamas, but admits that he got a bit hot wearing them in the Great Hall, which often had fires lit in the fireplaces. The students wore pointed hats that could fold up and be put in their pocket. Another pocket would hold their wand, although Makovsky admits that even she could never figure out how to put it in or take it out quickly.

PRECEDING PAGE: *Bonnie Wright sports Quidditch wear from* Harry Potter and the Half-Blood Prince *as she's filmed before a green-screen;* INSET: *The Hogwarts crest;* ABOVE: *Hermione, Ron, and Harry in first years robes and scarves in* Harry Potter and the Sorcerer's Stone; RIGHT: *Gryffindor robes for Harry Potter and the Chamber of Secrets;* TOP: *Harry and Hermione wearing the redesigned robes and scarves in* Harry Potter and the Goblet of Fire; OPPOSITE TOP: *Ties and crests for the four houses designed for* Sorcerer's Stone; OPPOSITE LEFT: *Costume reference for girl's uniform for* Sorcerer's Stone; OPPOSITE RIGHT: *Alfred Enoch (Dean Thomas) poses in scarf and robe for* Sorcerer's Stone.

"You two'd better change into your robes. I expect we'll be arriving soon."

Hermione Granger, *Harry Potter and the Sorcerer's Stone*

Jany Temime "changed the uniforms completely," she states, on *Harry Potter and the Prisoner of Azkaban*. The robes are fabricated out of wool, the shirts are 100 percent cotton, and the ties are now bigger and richer, made in a shiny silk. One of the most noticeable changes was that the pants, skirts, and sweaters are much darker, now black instead of the original gray. She placed the house colors in the lining of the robes, wanting to insure that each student's house could be seen clearly in their outfits, even across the Great Hall. The pointed hats were dropped and hoods were added, which Temime felt made the design "more urban. I wanted to make that link to the twenty-first century, as all kids have a hoodie." Another idea Temime had in concert with director Alfonso Cuarón was that, as the kids were getting older, "they would want to wear things their own way." She gave them the choice of interchangeable pieces, for example, a singlet or cardigan or oversized sweater, which would illustrate the personality of the child, and they were allowed to have shirts hanging out or loosened neckties (until Dolores Umbridge's tenure).

LEFT AND OPPOSITE: *Jany Temime's new costume designs for the student robes included more black and less gray, as seen in sketches by Laurent Guinci, as well as in a publicity photo featuring Devon Murray (Seamus Finnegan), Matthew Lewis (Neville Longbottom), and Alfred Enoch (Dean Thomas) for* Harry Potter and the Order of the Phoenix; ABOVE: *Goyle and Draco Malfoy pull up their hoods—now attached to the robes—in* Harry Potter and the Prisoner of Azkaban.

QUIDDITCH SPORTSWEAR

In *Harry Potter and the Sorcerer's Stone* and *Harry Potter and the Chamber of Secrets*, the Quidditch uniforms designed by Judianna Makovsky followed her "scholastic wizardry" philosophy, striving to evoke timelessness combined with familiarity. Sporting their house colors, the players wore crew-necked sweaters under a laced-up modified version of the school robes. Their white breeches bring fencing garb to mind, and their boots and arm and leg guards are reminiscent of nineteenth-century cricket and polo wear. The leg guards, made of thick leather with a canvas lining, had reinforced padded knees with a softer leather cover and buckles on the back. And, Makovsky recalls, "We discussed at length whether to have wizard gowns or not, but they flutter nicely and they *are* in the book."

As the films became darker and the Quidditch play became rougher, the uniforms were redesigned. For *Harry Potter and the Prisoner of Azkaban*, Jany Temime wanted to update the outfits so that they were more relatable to kids who were fans of present-day sports. Given that the Quidditch game took place in stormy weather, she chose a water-resistant nylon fabric and added goggles that helped modernize the look. She also added piping and numbers to the backs of the robes, though these were assigned randomly. Faster and more defensive play encouraged a redesign to ensure comfort and safety as the actors sat on their broomstick rigs, harnessed in front of a green screen. Unseen under their robes, bicycle-type seats were affixed to the brooms, gussets were added to seams, and padding was added to the backside of the costume.

Harry Potter and the Half-Blood Prince brought what director David Yates called "comedy Quidditch," when Ron Weasley tries out and makes the Gryffindor team. For the Quidditch trials, the students wear what Temime describes as a warm-up suit featuring sleeveless tunics over gray hoodies, now sporting numbers that indicated a specific position. "Each number tells which position you are playing, whether you're a Beater or a Seeker or

APPEARANCES:
Harry Potter and the Sorcerer's Stone
Harry Potter and the Chamber of Secrets
Harry Potter and the Prisoner of Azkaban
Harry Potter and the Goblet of Fire
Harry Potter and the Half-Blood Prince

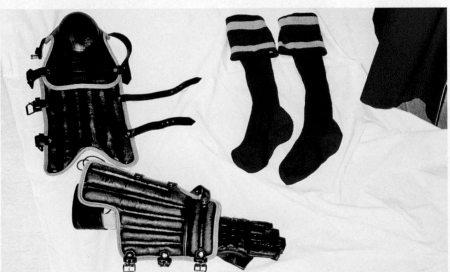

ABOVE: *Jany Temime's update to the Quidditch uniform included stronger arm and leg guards based on 1930s American football wear;* RIGHT: *Costume reference shot of Gryffindor uniform, second years;* OPPOSITE TOP LEFT: *Oliver Wood (Sean Biggerstaff), Gryffindor captain;* OPPOSITE TOP RIGHT: *Jany Temime designed Quidditch practice wear for* Harry Potter and the Half-Blood Prince, *sketch by Laurent Guinci;* OPPOSITE BOTTOM: *A clash of Slytherins and Gryffindors from* Chamber of Secrets. FOLLOWING PAGES: *Harry and Draco chase after the Golden snitch in artwork by Adam Brockbank.*

"Rough game, Quidditch."

"Brutal. But nobody's died in years!"

George and Fred Weasley, *Harry Potter and the Sorcerer's Stone*

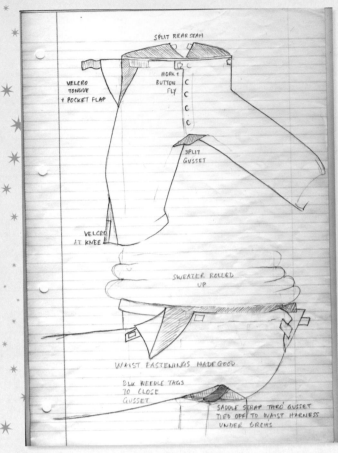

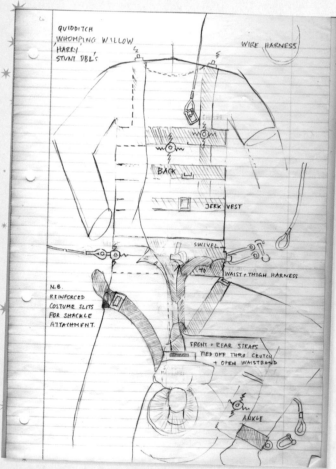

a Keeper," explains Temime. "In tryouts, you put on the number of the position you want." Keepers were 2, Seekers were 7. During the game, the wool sweaters were now covered by a streamlined lightweight tunic protected by shoulder, arm, and leg guards. These were created from pieces of leather that were soaked in water and then placed in a mold. Special attention was paid toward designing the safety gear with multiple articulations so that no guard piece locked to another during the intricate stunts. The molds proved beneficial when costumer Steve Kill was asked to create a pile of uniform pieces seen during Quidditch trials; these were produced in a foam rubber plastic. Helmets were added to the uniforms, based on early American football gear. Temime wanted to give the Slytherin robes more of a militaristic feel, and so, to a darker green than seen in previous uniforms, she added silver stripes and black stars. Additionally, the inside of their robes was lined with a shiny material to make them appear more luxurious.

The proportions of the Quidditch uniforms were played around with depending on the character. Actors Rupert Grint, as Gryffindor Keeper Ron Weasley, and Freddie Stroma, as wannabe Keeper Cormac McLaggen, are roughly physically the same size; the filmmakers wanted Stroma to appear bigger. Stroma's shoulder guards were scaled up, and extra panels were added to the front and back of his uniform to give him a bigger silhouette. In contrast, and because Ron once again ends up with hand-me-downs, his uniform was constructed on the small side, and sandpaper was used to scuff up the leather and laces.

And for the first time in the films, fan wear was created for the nonplaying students to support their teams. These were "branded" with the Hogwarts seal upon one of the four house colors on track-style T-shirts and hooded sweatshirts, accompanied by sweat pants in grays and blacks.

LEFT AND TOP LEFT: *Diagrams explain the Quidditch costumes' redesign for comfort, and methods of harnessing the outfits for stunts;* TOP RIGHT: *Hufflepuff uniform for* Harry Potter and the Prisoner of Azkaban, *sketch by Laurent Guinci;* OPPOSITE TOP: *New Slytherin and Gryffindor practice wear for* Harry Potter and the Half-Blood Prince *was designed for more aggressive play; drawn by Mauricio Carneiro;* OPPOSITE BOTTOM LEFT: *Freddie Stroma and Rupert Grint in front of a blue-screened practice pitch;* OPPOSITE BOTTOM CENTER: *Ginny, Harry, and Hermione try to calm Ron's pre-game jitters;* OPPOSITE BOTTOM RIGHT: *Post-game celebrations showcase the "branded" fan wear Temime created for* Half-Blood Prince.

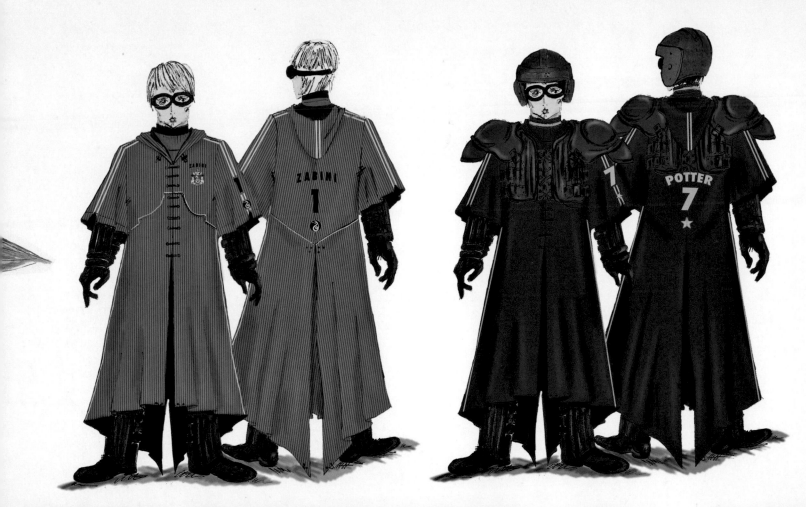

Chapter 4

THE TRIWIZARD TOURNAMENT

HOGWARTS
HARRY POTTER

PRECEDING PAGE: *Harry Potter in the maze for the third task of the Triwizard Tournament;* INSET: *Daniel Radcliffe in a publicity photo for Harry Potter and the Goblet of Fire;* TOP LEFT, BELOW, AND OPPOSITE TOP: *Jany Temime's designs for the three Triwizard Tournament tasks needed to accommodate broom-flying and swimming, sketches by Mauricio Carneiro;* ABOVE: *Harry in the dragon arena for the first task;* OPPOSITE BOTTOM: *Artwork by Dermot Power of the placement of special-effects gills that result from Harry's ingestion of gillyweed for the second task.*

What people don't realize," says Jany Temime, "is that there isn't just one costume for Harry—he has doubles and stunt doubles, and so you have multiples of the costume. We had five different stages of dragon costumes, from a clean version when he first enters, to a fully destroyed one at the end of the scene, so in total there were more than thirty-five dragon costumes just for Harry." A team of breakdown artists used sandpaper, lighters, and other tools to create the appearance of Harry's encounter with the fire-breathing Hungarian Horntail.

The makeup and hair departments were particularly challenged by the second task of the Triwizard Tournament. In addition to scars placed on Daniel Radcliffe's shoulders that came from Harry's combat with the dragon in the first task, the diving mask the actor wore between scenes in order to keep his eyes from becoming bloodshot underwater fitted exactly over the lightning bolt scar on his forehead. In order to keep the scar from coming off to a minimum, Amanda Knight and her crew developed a more sturdy waterproof makeup. "It did come off a few times," recalls Knight, "so we had to get him out on a few occasions to get the scar back on. But whatever happened to him in the tank was out of our control. We'd just stand by the side there, twitching."

→ *2 yellow stripes* ←

Another challenge was for Nick Dudman's team to give Harry the webbed hands and feet that materialize after he ingests Gillyweed. The fins were created easily as a molded prosthetic attached to Radcliffe's feet, containing a semi-rigid interior and a soft, flexible exterior that dovetailed into his ankles. In post-production, his ankles and heels were removed digitally.

The webbed hands took a bit more experimentation. The first attempt was to attach webbed material between Radcliffe's fingers, but this came off when his hands powered through the water while swimming. The second try was to use a thin webbed glove, which stayed on, but made the actor's hands look stubby. Length was added to the gloves, which made his hands look too big. The solution came when one of the crewmembers in the art finishing department was spotted washing a pair of nylon tights. "Her hand was stretched under the water, with the tights pulled up on her arm," Dudman explains. "But you couldn't actually see the tights on her hand." So a pair of tights was stretched over Radcliffe's hands and pulled up to under his tank top. Glue was applied between his fingers and the two layers of nylon were pressed together. "I think that was one of the cleverest theatrical tricks I've ever seen," says Dudman.

Radcliffe's costume for the task sported Gryffindor house's scarlet on the top when seen above the lake, but when under the waterline, another illusion came into play. Filming in fresh or saltwater changes the color of clothing; in this case, the red would be perceived as a dark brown, and so the top Radcliffe wore underwater was actually orange.

HOGWARTS
CEDRIC DIGGORY

"Cedric's a pretty nice guy," says actor Robert Pattinson, who plays the Hogwarts Triwizard Tournament champion in *Harry Potter and the Goblet of Fire*. "He plays fair. And he sticks to the rules, like he should." But, as Pattinson admits, "It's actually quite a lot of pressure playing the nice guy! And you know what they say about nice guys . . ." Director Mike Newell was particular about his casting of the part. "I knew that Cedric was going to die and I knew that in dying he would be very important to the story. I wanted him to be one of those clearly sacrificial figures, like the ultimate fighter pilot. And that's absolutely one of the things that Robert's got available. He's glorious-looking, and he does have that sort of posh doom about him."

For the champions' costumes for the Triwizard Tournament, Jany Temime chose synthetic fabrics that would be tough and durable during the three tasks, taking her cue from her redesign of the Quidditch uniforms for *Harry Potter and the Prisoner of Azkaban*. The design of the Hogwarts costumes was the same for both Harry and Cedric, just in their house's different colors. Multiple versions were required, though, as the various stunts took their toll on the outfits. The stunts during the three tasks were challenging for the actors, but Pattinson says that jumping out of the tree for his first appearance in the film "was a nightmare. It really takes it out on your knees after a while, jumping some twelve feet or so. The first one was quite fun. But after a while, my knees got very stiff very quickly. I think by the final take it really showed in my expression when I landed!"

INSET AND OPPOSITE: *Robert Pattinson as Hufflepuff champion Cedric Diggory;* RIGHT: *Costume designs for Cedric's champion's wear by Jany Temime, sketches by Mauricio Carneiro for* Harry Potter and the Goblet of Fire.

APPEARANCE:
Harry Potter and the Goblet of Fire

HOUSE:
Hufflepuff

OCCUPATION:
Hogwarts student, Triwizard Tournament Champion, Hufflepuff Seeker

CEDRIC'S WAND

Cedric Diggory's black-tipped baton-style wand is wrapped around with wheel-like designs and alchemical symbols etched at the handle.

BEAUXBATONS
MADAME MAXIME

When asked to describe her character of the Beauxbatons headmistress, Madame Olympe Maxime, Frances de la Tour states: "She's a teacher who loves her girls and dresses them all beautifully. And she just happens to be big." After a pause, de la Tour continues, "She's in serious denial about being big."

When Jany Temime met with de la Tour, the actress reiterated the character's philosophy of "I'm not big" and even asked if the character could appear thin. "But I told her, 'No, you are a giant, you are big. A big presence, but an elegant one. You will never be a tiny little thing. So think formidable,' says Temime. "She is a woman who wants to be seen." Madame Maxime's elegant clothing inspired Eithne Fennell to give the headmistress chic hair styles to complement the outfits. "We thought a simple bob would do, but to give her a bit more flair, we'd streak her hair with different colors to go with her outfits."

To play Madame Maxime at her most gigantic, seven-foot-tall basketball player and film actor Ian Whyte was scaled up to eight foot four by wearing stilts with high heels. So in addition to the problems inherent in scaling up clothing prints, Temime needed to ensure that Madame Maxime's outfits were floor length to cover the stilts, and had long sleeves in order to seamlessly disguise the transitions to her double's fake hands. To camouflage the attachment point for Maxime's silicon animatronic head, Temime used faux fur collars and cuffs, feathered neck pieces, and even large ruffs. In addition to learning to walk on the stilts, Whyte needed to learn to waltz with Martin Bayfield, Hagrid's double, for the Yule Ball.

FIRST APPEARANCE:
Harry Potter and the Goblet of Fire

ADDITIONAL APPEARANCE:
Harry Potter and the Deathly Hallows – Part 1

OCCUPATION:
Beauxbatons Headmistress

INSET: *Frances de la Tour as Madame Maxime;* LEFT AND OPPOSITE TOP LEFT: *Madame Maxime and Hagrid dance at the Yule Ball in* Harry Potter and the Goblet of Fire *and a sketch of Madame Maxime's outfit;* ABOVE AND OPPOSITE BOTTOM LEFT AND CENTER: *An assortment of suits and separates, all sketched by Mauricio Carneiro;* OPPOSITE TOP RIGHT: *The Beauxbatons girls' entrance in* Goblet of Fire; OPPOSITE BOTTOM RIGHT: *Madame Maxime's outfits required high collars.*

"Blimey, that's one big woman."

Seamus Finnegan, *Harry Potter and the Goblet of Fire*

Madame Maxime's animatronic head was equipped with a performance control device that activated the mouth's movement as Whyte delivered dialogue from inside. This helped to cue the other actors. The other facial expressions and eye movements were controlled by Nick Dudman's crew. "But there are always shots where you must have the actor's performance," Dudman explains, "where you want to start close on her face, pull out, and reveal her size. Then you'd blue screen her." In other instances, Dudman used inventive ways to create the illusion of height when shooting close-ups of de la Tour. "We used smaller sets, cheated angles, and sometimes we just put her on a pile of boards that raised her up. When you see the film, you should think, 'My God, that woman is tall.' And if we can achieve that, then it's a job well done."

BEAUXBATONS
FLEUR DELACOUR AND THE BEAUXBATONS GIRLS

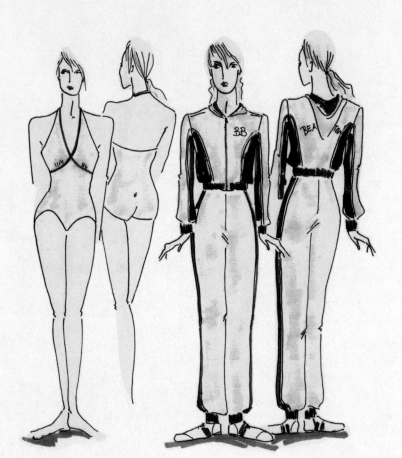

FIRST APPEARANCE:
Harry Potter and the Goblet of Fire

ADDITIONAL APPEARANCES OF FLEUR:
Harry Potter and the Deathly Hallows – Part 1
Harry Potter and the Deathly Hallows – Part 2

OCCUPATION:
Beauxbatons student,
Triwizard Tournament Champion

Clémence Poesy, who plays Fleur Delacour, feels that the Beauxbatons girls made an impressive entrance into the Great Hall of Hogwarts in *Harry Potter and the Goblet of Fire*, "But I wanted to switch with the Durmstrang boys, as least once, and come in doing their stuff." Poesy was an avid fan of the Harry Potter novels, and has strong opinions about the character she plays. "In a way, she's what the English think a French girl would be. She's chic, and graceful, and very serious, but she's also Miss Perfect. I saw her as the kind of girl I used to hate in high school!" she ends with a laugh. "She's not a cliché, but she embodies many French clichés."

Jany Temime attended a French boarding school when she was young and remembers, "It was very important that we were always wearing the same thing. And we were quite happy to do it, which I think is the

big difference with English children, because when they have a uniform the first thing they do is to try to find a way to change it." She brought another personal observation from being French into the design of the costumes—that of the cold Scotland climate. "In Scotland they wear wool, and even if it's a beautiful wool it's still wool. It's practical and it keeps you warm. So then the French girls arrive wearing silk, completely unaware of the climate in Scotland, completely impractical, which I thought was great." For their outfits, Temime chose a fabric in what is known as "French blue," as it would stand out from the blacks, browns, and grays of the other students' muted palette. Pointed hats that resemble a wizardy version of a Trilby hat and a short cape complete an outfit with either a short dress or a short jacketed suit.

FLEUR'S WAND

Fleur Delacour's wand boasts an intricately carved design at the handle, and a long leaf that wraps itself around the shaft.

INSET AND OPPOSITE RIGHT: *Clémence Poésy as Beauxbatons champion Fleur Delacour;* OPPOSITE TOP LEFT: *Fleur's Triwizard Tournament outfits, sketch by Mauricio Carneiro;* ABOVE: *Madame Maxime follows her Beauxbatons charges into the Great Hall in* Harry Potter and the Goblet of Fire; LEFT: *Sketches by Mauricio Carneiro of Jany Temime's designs for Gabrielle Delacour (left and right) and the not-very-warm French blue Beauxbatons uniform (center).* SIDEBAR: *Artwork of Fleur's wand by Ben Dennett.*

DURMSTRANG
IGOR KARKAROFF

Though not as tall as his counterpart at Beauxbatons, Igor Karkaroff, the headmaster of Durmstrang Institute, who appears in *Harry Potter and the Goblet of Fire*, is formidable in his own way. "I think he acts very dramatically and even arrogantly," says Serbian actor Predrag Bjelac, "but it's because of his past. He's trying to appear to be what he was before the trials, someone on top of things, but, really, he knows he's not on top anymore." Karkaroff's past is that of a convicted Death Eater who gives up Barty Crouch Jr. in exchange for freedom. Seen in a Pensieve flashback, Bjelac is dressed in the rags of an Azkaban prisoner. His look was adjusted with fake colored teeth—"Of course they're not mine!" Bjelac declares—and a beard he grew for the part was given extensions, "but my hair is always like that," he laughs. The actor admits to feeling claustrophobic while encased in the Iron Maiden–like cage he sat in for a week of filming, but used the fear to enhance his performance.

APPEARANCE:
Harry Potter and the Goblet of Fire

OCCUPATION:
Head of Durmstrang Institute

MEMBER OF:
Death Eaters

Igor Karkaroff, *Harry Potter*
and the Goblet of Fire

INSET AND OPPOSITE RIGHT: *Predrag Bjelac*
as Durmstrang Headmaster Igor Karkaroff;
OPPOSITE BOTTOM LEFT: *Karkaroff*
and Professor McGonagall at the Triwizard
Tournament opening banquet in Harry Potter
and the Goblet of Fire; LEFT: Sketches by
Mauricio Carneiro of Jany Temime's designs for
Karkaroff's coat; BELOW: Igor Karkaroff and
his aide (Tolga Safer) arrive in the Great Hall.

DURMSTRANG
VIKTOR KRUM AND THE DURMSTRANG BOYS

Actor Stanislav Ianevski considers his casting in the role of Durmstrang champion (and "Bulgarian bonbon") Viktor Krum "a Hollywood fairy tale. I was running down a hall at school and the casting director heard me shouting to someone and she asked me to audition." There is irony that the sound of Ianevski's voice led him in the direction of the role of a character he describes as "more of a physical being than a talkative one." Furthermore, Ianevski, who is originally from Bulgaria, had been living in England for several years and had lost any distinctive native inflections. "For the film, Viktor Krum really isn't good at English. So I do go back to a rough, tough Bulgarian accent."

Jany Temime provided a strong Slavic flavor to warm woolen clothing for the "sons of Durmstrang," a wizarding school set in a northern European clime. Unlike the Beauxbatons girls, the boys are dressed for winter in high-collared fur-lined coats. The top of Karkaroff's staff and the coats' belt buckles feature the double-headed eagle that is the coat of arms for Durmstrang, while buttons resemble talons of these raptor birds grasping the thick material. The students wear variations on the traditional Russian *ushanka* cap, with its round crown and earflaps, and the *shapka* hat, with its peaked top. Temime thought of Durmstrang in terms of a military-type school, and so the clothes are more utilitarian and, unlike the Hogwarts students, the boys were not given the option of individuality. Additionally, Eithne Fennell notes that "The boys' hair was clipped every other day," to keep it consistently short. Ianevski credits the clothing for helping him shape his character. "I wear a very big and hot coat. But once I have it on I forget about the heat. I become more powerful and focused. As soon as I put that big coat on, I feel pimped out, as the Americans say."

FIRST APPEARANCE:
Harry Potter and the Goblet of Fire

ADDITIONAL APPEARANCE OF VIKTOR:
Harry Potter and the Deathly Hallows – Part 1
(deleted from film)

OCCUPATION:
Durmstrang student,
Bulgarian National Quidditch Team Seeker,
Triwizard Tournament Champion

KRUM'S WAND

The eagle that serves as a symbol of the Durmstrang Institute is echoed in the kestrel bird's head sculpted on the handle of Viktor Krum's wand. The light wood, with a natural curve to it, is roughly carved.

"Mostly he watches me study. It's a bit annoying actually."

Hermione Granger, *Harry Potter and the Goblet of Fire*

INSET AND BELOW: *Stanislav Ianevski as Durmstrang champion Viktor Krum;* OPPOSITE RIGHT: *Krum is flanked by Headmaster Karkaroff and his aide upon his entrance into the Great Hall in Harry Potter and the Goblet of Fire;* OPPOSITE BOTTOM: *Artwork by Adam Brockbank for Goblet of Fire;* LEFT: *Three different iterations of student coats—all very warm;* BELOW LEFT: *Viktor's Triwizard Tournament champion's wear was decorated with the double-headed eagle insignia of the school, all sketches by Mauricio Carneiro.*

RITA SKEETER

When Jany Temime began to design the outfits that *Daily Prophet* reporter Rita Skeeter would wear during the events of the Triwizard Tournaments tasks, she noticed that "gossip journalists always seem to coordinate with the occasion. If they're at Ascot, they wear a hat; if they're at a car race, they wear a leather jacket." Rita Skeeter's attire was designed so that she always matched the story she was reporting, and actress Miranda Richardson agreed with the idea, believing that "It's as much of a duty to her to look right for the occasion as it is to tell the truth—as she sees it —for her readership." Temime was initially inspired by the Hollywood gossip columnists from the 1940s, who dressed as extravagantly as the stars they interviewed, but a consultation with Richardson encouraged her to explore the "business" side of Skeeter's reporting. Richardson felt that Skeeter thought constantly about increasing not only her sales but her notoriety. "Rita Skeeter wants power," Temime explains. "She has a cruel thirst for it, and Miranda wanted to bring out a touch of madness in her look that displayed this, so we switched to suits."

Skeeter's clear "poison pen" approach to journalism is reflected in the outfit she wears during her first meeting with the school champions; Temime refers to the color as "acidic green. If it was a liquid, it would be poisonous, you'd better not drink it!" The collar and cuffs of what Temime calls one of her favorite outfits are adorned in a bold pink faux fur. The champions' first challenge finds Rita decked out in a high-booted,

INSET: *Miranda Richardson as Rita Skeeter;* BELOW: *Skeeter's outfit for the Triwizard Tournament's first task—dragons—is appropriately reptilian as seen in the film and in original sketches for* Harry Potter and the Goblet of Fire; *FAR RIGHT AND OPPOSITE CENTER: Jany Temime's concept for the dress she fabricated in an "acidic green," worn during Skeeter's initial introduction to the champions, Cedric Diggory and Harry Potter;* OPPOSITE TOP LEFT AND OPPOSITE BOTTOM LEFT: *The journalist's ensembles for the second and third tasks, all sketches by Mauricio Carneiro.*

APPEARANCE:
Harry Potter and the Goblet of Fire

OCCUPATION:
Reporter for the *Daily Prophet*, author of
The Life and Lies of Albus Dumbledore

ADDITIONAL SKILL SET:
Animagus

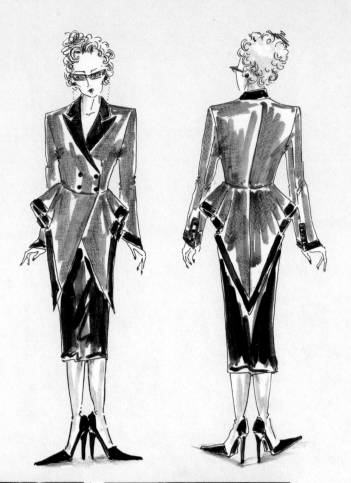

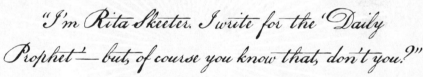

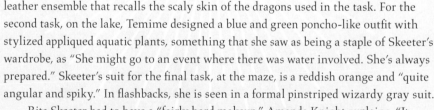

"I'm Rita Skeeter. I write for the 'Daily Prophet'—but, of course you know that, don't you?"

Rita Skeeter, *Harry Potter and the Goblet of Fire*

leather ensemble that recalls the scaly skin of the dragons used in the task. For the second task, on the lake, Temime designed a blue and green poncho-like outfit with stylized appliqued aquatic plants, something that she saw as being a staple of Skeeter's wardrobe, as "She might go to an event where there was water involved. She's always prepared." Skeeter's suit for the final task, at the maze, is a reddish orange and "quite angular and spiky." In flashbacks, she is seen in a formal pinstriped wizardy gray suit.

Rita Skeeter had to have a "fairly hard makeup," Amanda Knight explains. "It wasn't to be a soft, alluring look, but Miranda was really game for whatever we planned for her, and came in with some ideas of her own." Richardson endured the character's long nails, but drew the line at Skeeter's gold teeth, mentioned in the novel. Miranda Richardson and Mike Newell opted instead for dentures embedded with a diamond.

It took three tries to get the right hair color for the character. "We tried brown, we tried red, we tried really dark," says Eithne Fennel. "Then we just realized it had to be blonde." Fennel agreed that Skeeter's hairstyles, just as her outfits, would be dictated by the event. "In general, we wanted her basic look to be like her hair had just come out of rollers. But with the dragons, we put a headband on her with horns in it. By the lakeside, her hair flowed a little more. So each time you saw her, she had a different hairdo." Richardson was pleased with the overall look of the character. "Rita has a wonderful old-fashioned glamour," she says, "and she certainly won't go missing in a room!"

Chapter 5

Chapter 5

CELEBRATIONS

THE YULE BALL

Director Mike Newell described the Yule Ball in *Harry Potter and the Goblet of Fire* as "a film within a film, complicated but fun." Jany Temime was tasked with creating hundreds of gowns and robes, and felt it was most important for their outfits "to show their personalities," she says. "Especially as they're now teenagers with the opportunity to make a fashion statement."

For the boys' dress robes, Temime wanted something that was a reinterpretation of their daily black robes designed for formal evening wear, which she calls a "wizard tuxedo." The robes are made from a shiny material with satin collars that can flip up (no hoods), usually paired with a black waistcoat or vest. "Once you're in that costume, with that cloak," says Robert Pattinson, "you do feel a lot more elegant." Very few differences were allowed: Slytherins wore a white bow tie, "because they think it's posh," says Temime, but most others wore black; the shirt buttons would vary; and the waistcoats bore a few different patterns. The Weasley twins wore individually styled waistcoats that bore signs of their mother's crafty hands. The exception to this rule, and perhaps winner of the "worst dressed" award, was Ron Weasley, who received a set of hand-me-down dress robes.

"Poor Ron," says Temime. "The robes are so wrong but at the same time, he's so adorable." Temime wanted to evoke sympathy for her favorite character to costume. "We knew they were something that had been around for twenty years or more, stuffed away in a closet, just nasty." She found a carpet-like fabric that had "amazing organic designs" that appealed to her, a tweed waistcoat, "and then we just went mad with it," liberally applying old lace and other ornamentation. "It's just horrible," says Rupert Grint. "It's covered in flowers and pink lace and it's so girly that I originally think it must be for Ginny." Temime gave it that hint of girlishness on purpose. "I thought, it's so important for a young man to be dressed as a young man, the most ridiculous thing I could do was give it a slight feminine touch, to add to the shame. But because it's so wrong, there's something touching about it. I think another reason you love Ron is through his bad clothes."

PRECEDING PAGE: *Hermione Granger dances with Viktor Krum at the Yule Ball in* Harry Potter and the Goblet of Fire; TOP LEFT: *Harry Potter and Ron Weasley wear very contrasting formal robes, also seen in costume illustrations (top and above);* OPPOSITE LEFT AND CENTER: *Costume illustrations and a publicity photo showcase Hermione's beautiful gown, all sketches by Mauricio Carneiro;* OPPOSITE RIGHT: *Katie Leung as Cho Chang, Cedric Diggory's date for the Ball.*

"I remember that the first time Emma walked on the set," recalls Eithne Fennell, "when we were doing a tryout, the whole crew gasped. It was like an intake of breath, because she looked so gorgeous." Jany Temime compares Hermione Granger's transformation for the Ball to that of an emerging butterfly, "So I wanted something that was light and would float about her as she went down the stairs." Temime felt that a girl who has been a bit of a tomboy would dream of wearing something romantic and princess-like, but did not want her to look too womanly, and it took several designs before she felt she had achieved the right balance. The dress is constructed of more than twelve yards of silk and chiffon, all stitched by hand; Temime insisted it be a rose pink. Four dresses needed to be made, two for Emma Watson and two for her doubles. "The gown was absolutely gorgeous," says Watson, "and I was absolutely terrified I was going to rip it or spill something on it. I literally would not sit down in it. I wouldn't walk in until I had to because I was so worried I was going to wreck it. I'd never worn anything so beautiful." The moment when Hermione comes down the staircase was a highly pressured one. "I was so nervous about the whole thing, because it was such an anticipated moment." After a few rehearsals, they went for a first take. "So I walked down about three steps and then fell down in front of the whole set, which was incredibly embarrassing." Getting that out of her system, Watson's next takes brought the enchantment of that moment. "It was great for Hermione," Watson adds, "because she's never had anybody look at her in that way before. She's got the brains, and in this one, you know, she looks nice in a beautiful dress. If she can do it, anyone can."

Temime had other female students to dress, including Cho Chang, Harry's crush and Cedric Diggory's date. "I wanted something with a Chinese influence for Cho Chang," says Temime, and dressed her in a long satin ivory-colored dress with hanging sleeves and a capelet with a Mandarin collar, all appliqued with lace peony flowers. The Patil twins, Harry and Ron's dates for the ball, wore complementary saris in bright pink and orange. Ginny wore a pastel-colored gown in light green

and pink, with a lace-edged collar and star-shaped decorations that was appropriate for her young age. "Though," says Bonnie Wright, "I have a feeling Mum adapted an old dress that maybe she'd worn in the fifties." Temime wanted the Beauxbatons girls "to appear allied," and so dressed them in varying shades of gray. Fleur Delacour's dress contained about sixty meters (131 feet) of chiffon in her pleated gown, edged with "witchy lace flowers." More than one hundred extra workers were needed to sew and embellish the three hundred ball gowns created for the girls. The Durmstrang boys were outfitted in an Eastern European–type uniform with large silver buckles and a short fur-lined cape draped over one shoulder that flared out while dancing.

The staff from Hogwarts and the other schools also dressed up for the occasion. Dumbledore's gown was gold and silver, and Karkaroff's robe was in white. Professor McGonagall's gown was a deep green, with high pointed shoulders, and lapels and sleeves draping from her elbows, constructed using a special pleating technique. Madame Maxime wore a long ecru gown with Dolman sleeves as she danced with Hagrid, who wore his striped mohair suit. Severus Snape wore his usual black coat.

During the shoot for the Yule Ball, an assembly line of hair and makeup people was put together to ready the hundreds of teenage actors. For logistical reasons, the actors were separated into their respective schools. "I employed twenty-five people in different areas," recalls Eithne Fennell. "Four people just doing the updos on the Beauxbatons girls." The work was done in shifts; swapping groups in and out of school sessions. This "night of well-mannered frivolity," as Professor McGonagall describes it, was the first opportunity to show the maturing students with a new sophistication. "The kids loved it, we loved it," says Amanda Knight, "and it looked fabulous."

TOP LEFT AND TOP RIGHT: *Costume illustrations for Ginny Weasley's dress and Fleur Delacour's gown for Harry Potter and the Goblet of Fire;* CENTER: *Cedric Diggory and Cho Chang at the Ball;* BOTTOM: *Even the professors brought out their formal wear;* OPPOSITE: *Publicity photo of the Triwizard Tournament champions' formal wear—Stanislav Ianevski (Viktor Krum) wearing a red coat with talon-shaped fasteners and fur cape, Clémence Poésy (Fleur Delacour) in more than 100 yards of chiffon, and Robert Pattinson (Cedric Diggory) in "tuxedo-style" robes.*

PROFESSOR SLUGHORN'S CHRISTMAS PARTY

Horace Slughorn's reinstatement at Hogwarts in *Harry Potter and the Half-Blood Prince* also revived the parties he had hosted in years past. For his Christmas party, the outfit Jany Temime created for the professor featured velour slacks, a textured suit jacket and vest, tassels, and a sleeveless robe imprinted with an Asian pattern. Temime worked with production designer Stuart Craig and set decorator Stephenie McMillan to ensure that the room's décor did not overpower the costumes, or vice versa, as both needed to reflect the eccentricity of Slughorn's personality.

Two years after the Yule Ball in *Harry Potter and the Goblet of Fire*, Temime enjoyed another chance to create formal evening wear for the students and teachers. The boys are back in their dress robes, but as "It's not a grand party," Temime explains, "each wears a smart shirt and tie, with very elegant black trousers." Harry Potter's suit features a plum shirt, a color that Temime slowly introduced into his wardrobe for the final films.

The girls take advantage of the occasion to glam up in their individual ways. Hermione Granger's dress is reminiscent of her Yule Ball gown in *Harry Potter and the Goblet of Fire,* but this time in a pale salmon pink, tailored taffeta knee-length that Temime refers to as her "prom" dress. For Ginny, Temime wanted to show the "beautiful young girl who caught the heart of Harry Potter." She felt that though Mrs. Weasley is still making Ginny's clothes, with this dress, "She would aim it to have a bit of fantasy. A bit of mystery. And be very romantic." Temime designed the dress to have elegance within its simple structure. Produced in lush velvet and silk, its turquoise and black colors diverge from the traditional Weasley palette. Temime recalls that when Bonnie Wright (Ginny) appeared on the set, "and everything lit her, I thought it was really a pretty moment."

Perhaps no ensemble is more character-defining than Luna Lovegood's "Christmas tree" dress. Luna is described as wearing "silver spangled robes" in *Harry Potter and the Half-Blood Prince*, but, as Evanna Lynch perceives it, "I doubt she goes to many of these kinds of things, so she's using this opportunity to dress up, as she imagines it, properly." The mauve and silver layered dress is complemented by silver slippers, silver stockings, and a silver bracelet featuring a silver-and-white beaded hare, representing Luna's Patronus, crafted by Lynch. "It is completely mad, but it's her," Temime states.

Neville Longbottom is also at the party, as a member of the wait staff, wearing what actor Matthew Lewis describes as a costume that "looked like he should work on the Titanic. Everything was very white, with gold braiding on the shoulders, like a sailor's. They even had a silly matching hat." The actor felt that Neville was just happy to be at the party, and Lewis was just as happy that he didn't end up having to wear the hat.

INSET: *Evanna Lynch as Luna Lovegood;* RIGHT: *Luna Lovegood's dress, designed by Jany Temime, fit the Christmas theme of the party in* Harry Potter and the Half-Blood Prince; TOP RIGHT: *Ginny Weasley arrives at the party;* OPPOSITE TOP RIGHT: *Luna with the vampire Sanguini (Charlie Bennison) and Eldred Worple (Paul Ritter);* OPPOSITE TOP LEFT: *Professor Slughorn and photographer Adrian;* OPPOSITE BOTTOM: *Harry Potter greets the* Titanically *attired Neville Longbottom.*

Chapter 6

THE ORDER OF
THE PHOENIX

James & Lily Potter

JAMES POTTER

FIRST APPEARANCE:
Harry Potter and the Sorcerer's Stone

ADDITIONAL APPEARANCES:
Harry Potter and the Chamber of Secrets
Harry Potter and the Prisoner of Azkaban
Harry Potter and the Goblet of Fire
Harry Potter and the Order of the Phoenix
Harry Potter and the Deathly Hallows – Part 1
Harry Potter and the Deathly Hallows – Part 2

HOUSE:
Gryffindor

MEMBER OF:
Order of the Phoenix

ADDITIONAL SKILL SET:
Animagus ("Prongs," a stag)

PATRONUS:
Stag

Throughout the course of the films, Harry Potter is given glances of his parents, James and Lily, through the Mirror of Erised in *Harry Potter and the Sorcerer's Stone*, and in photos given to him in *Harry Potter and the Chamber of Secrets*, *Harry Potter and the Prisoner of Azkaban*, and *Harry Potter and the Order of the Phoenix*. In their adult years, James and Lily are always fashionably dressed, but modestly and casually, in muted colors and classic tailoring.

While at Hogwarts, James belonged to an earlier group affectionately known as the Marauders. These Gryffindor students, who include Sirius Black and Peter Pettigrew, learned to become Animagi to help their fourth member and friend—Remus Lupin, a werewolf. These young wizards band together, and for *Harry Potter and the Prisoner of Azkaban* director Alfonso Cuarón, "band" was the operative word. Initially, the Marauders were to be seen in a flashback in the movie, and so Cuarón gave some thought as to who they were and what they looked like. "I was adamant about grounding everything, including the characters, in reality. When I read the books, for me it was very clear that the universe that J.K. Rowling wrote is not a precious one; I think it's very mischievous, even wicked." With that playful idea in mind, Cuarón looked to the Muggle world for inspiration on a group of four young men who had formed an alliance. "We had seen flashbacks of [Harry's] parents, and I thought that James was

PRECEDING PAGE: *Two members of the Order of the Phoenix: Mad-Eye Moody and Nymphadora Tonks (Natalia Tena);* INSET: *Adrian Rawlins as James Potter;* RIGHT: *Costume sketch for Lily Potter's dress worn in the* Order of the Phoenix *photo, sketch by Mauricio Carneiro;* TOP AND OPPOSITE: *The Marauders as envisioned by Adam Brockbank—(left to right) Remus Lupin, Sirius Black, James Potter, and Peter Pettigrew—and confronting Severus Snape (against the tree), by artist Andrew Williamson, both for Harry Potter and the Order of the Phoenix.*

actually a very cool dude. And this is when I started thinking that the flashbacks should look as if they were the Beatles, circa the late sixties/early seventies." Cuarón felt that James reminded him of John Lennon; Gary Oldman remembers the Fab Four equivalent a little differently, however. "James was like Paul—good looking and sure of himself—and Sirius was like John as he was a little bit reckless, a bit of an anarchic troublemaker." The Marauders weren't seen on-screen until *Harry Potter and the Order of the Phoenix*, but Cuarón's influence remained. James Potter wears round wireframe glasses and has a mop-top haircut; each of the Marauders has fledgling sideburns. Their Hogwarts robes of that earlier time have thinner collars and their trousers' waistlines are set lower on the hips.

Harry Potter and the Order of the Phoenix's titular group is seen in a photograph featuring a more mature group of Marauders surrounded by other members of the Order. Being a few years later, their clothes are firmly rooted in the seventies: midi-length peasant dresses embellished with velvet, Nehru collars, and fisherman's caps, albeit with a wizarly approach.

LILY POTTER

FIRST APPEARANCE:
Harry Potter and the Sorcerer's Stone

ADDITIONAL APPEARANCES:
Harry Potter and the Chamber of Secrets
Harry Potter and the Prisoner of Azkaban
Harry Potter and the Goblet of Fire
Harry Potter and the Order of the Phoenix
Harry Potter and the Half-Blood Prince
Harry Potter and the Deathly Hallows – Part 1
Harry Potter and the Deathly Hallows – Part 2

HOUSE:
Gryffindor

MEMBER OF:
Order of the Phoenix

PATRONUS:
Doe

OPPOSITE TOP: *A Pensieve memory of Severus Snape's in* Harry Potter and the Order of the Phoenix *shows the young Marauders in earlier versions of the Hogwarts robe—(left to right) Sirius/Padfoot (James Walters), James/Prongs (Robert Jarvis), Remus/Moony (James Utechin, middle back), and Peter/Wormtail (Charles Hughes);* OPPOSITE BOTTOM: *A sketch of young Lily Potter for* Harry Potter and the Deathly Hallows – Part 2 *wearing a design by Jany Temime, drawn by Mauricio Carneiro;* TOP LEFT AND ABOVE: *Another Pensieve memory of Snape's in* Deathly Hallows – Part 2 *shows young Lily Potter (Ellie Darcey-Alden) with young Snape (Benedict Clarke) at Hogwarts;* TOP RIGHT: *Harry Potter watches his parents—James (Robert Jarvis, left) and Lily (Susie Shinner)—as older Hogwarts students in a Pensieve memory in* Order of the Phoenix.

SIRIUS BLACK

T he first time you see me," says Gary Oldman of his appearance in *Harry Potter and the Prisoner of Azkaban*, "I've just escaped after twelve years in prison. So I'm pretty much a disheveled wreck, an undernourished guy in need of some dental work, a shave, and some decent clothes." Jany Temime spent some time thinking about how a prisoner in Azkaban would be dressed, and drafted several different possibilities, "But then I thought, a prisoner is a prisoner. A prisoner wears something dirty and striped. And that's it." Wide horizontal stripes were chosen for the pajama-style prisoner clothes, and Sirius wears a beaten-up coat that he picked up somewhere after his escape. There were also numerous tests for Sirius Black's hair. "We tried it short and long," recalls Oldman. "Very short gray hair, or almost bald with tufts of hair, like it was falling out. Bearded and not bearded. The book says he has long, greasy hair and that's what we ended up with." A scraggly gray beard and moustache were added. The makeup crew provided a set of rotten teeth, and covered his body in tattoos that featured runic and alchemical symbols, suggested by director Alfonso Cuarón. For his brief appearance in *Harry Potter and the Goblet of Fire*, seen in a fire's flames, Oldman was filmed in a cleaned-up version of the same long wig and facial hair.

Based on the look of Sirius Black and the other Marauders during their years at Hogwarts, in Cuarón's tip to the Beatles, the Sirius seen in *Harry Potter and the Order of the Phoenix* almost recaptures the glory of his youth. Now he sports a trimmed moustache and set of light mutton chops, reminiscent of John Lennon in late 1968. Jany Temime assumed that Black had kept his clothes at his Grimmauld Place home while he was in prison, and was wearing them again, although through

FIRST APPEARANCE:
Harry Potter and the Prisoner of Azkaban

ADDITIONAL APPEARANCES:
Harry Potter and the Goblet of Fire
Harry Potter and the Order of the Phoenix
Harry Potter and the Deathly Hallows – Part 2

HOUSE:
Gryffindor

OCCUPATION:
Fugitive

MEMBER OF:
Order of the Phoenix

ADDITIONAL SKILL SET:
Animagus ("Padfoot," a dog)

INSET AND OPPOSITE: *Gary Oldman as Sirius Black;* ABOVE: *A recently escaped Sirius meets up with fellow Marauder Remus Lupin in* Harry Potter and the Prisoner of Azkaban; RIGHT: *Jany Temime's design of Sirius's coat for* Harry Potter and the Order of the Phoenix, *sketch by Mauricio Carneiro.*

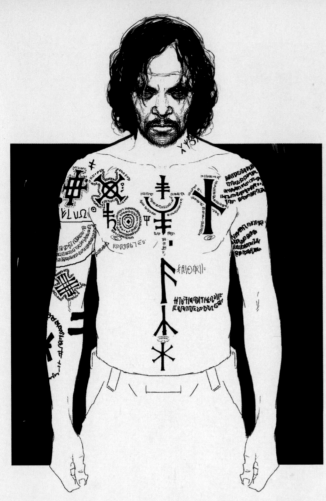

the course of time that had become a bit faded and moth-eaten. "He was a rock star then," says Temime. "He was popular and glamorous. I supposed that Sirius still had that wonderful wardrobe in his closet and would want to wear it again. And he wore it brilliantly, but of course, after being dressed in rags, whatever he wore would look fantastic." Sirius is dressed in crushed velvets, embroidered vests strung with gold watch chains, and a pair of low-heeled boots that Oldman deemed "fabulous." Typical of the late sixties time period, patterns were mixed and matched, and so Sirius wears a series of striped shirts and blazers that contrast with his vests and pants. The velvet waistcoat he wears in the Ministry of Magic battle was dyed and then a printing technique called "devore" was used to burn a pattern of roses into the fabric. These flowers were then painted to look like embroidery that had worn away over the years. Oldman admits, though, that "When you're up there in the Veil Room, wafting your wand, in double velvet, it gets hot. I was much cooler in the Azkaban prison wear."

SIRIUS'S WAND

Sirius Black's wand is simply shaped but highly decorated, and a combination of round and square. The shaft has a gentle, slow twist to it, decorated with a spiral line embellished with circular insets. These lead to a flattened handle adorned in runic symbols that complement the tattoos on Black's body. Actor Gary Oldman was instructed by wand battle choreographer Paul Harris to give his wand moves more of an angular, "street" feeling, which he thought befitted someone who had spent time in Azkaban. "It is similar in a way to fencing," says Oldman, "because there's blocks and deflections, you know. Defensive and attacking moves. Paul really created a language." In fact, five specific attack moves were devised, with names including "crux" (across the body) and "latros" (from behind the back).

"It's been fourteen years, and still a day doesn't go by I don't miss your dad."

Sirius Black, *Harry Potter and the Order of the Phoenix*

OPPOSITE LEFT: *Artist Rob Bliss documented Sirius's Russian-style tattoos;* OPPOSITE RIGHT: *Costume ideas for Sirius's Azkaban prisoner wear and the coat he picks up to hide it, in* Harry Potter and the Prisoner of Azkaban, *sketches by Laurent Guinci;* OPPOSITE BOTTOM AND TOP RIGHT: *Sketches by Mauricio Carneiro for* Harry Potter and the Order of the Phoenix *of Sirius's Seventies-style suits;* TOP LEFT: *Echoes of a young Sirius Black are seen in his revitalized wardrobe for* Order of the Phoenix; BELOW: *Sirius with his godson, Harry Potter, at King's Cross Station.*

NYMPHADORA TONKS

Natalia Tena admits that her first audition for the role of Nymphadora Tonks in *Harry Potter and the Order of the Phoenix* was pretty much a disaster. "I hadn't seen any of the films. I hadn't read any of the books. I didn't know what a Muggle was. I walked into the room and tripped over a chair, and for some reason, I was quite loud." Later that day, her agent called and told her, "Nat, it really *was* awful, but for some reason they want to see you again." After a long audition process, during which Tena read the books and movies that had come out, she landed the part. "I really did love stories with witches. Until I was six, I believed three witches had left me on the doorstep. On my eighteenth birthday, my mother gave me a broom, so perhaps this was meant to be." Director David Yates gave Tena an important note to follow: "Find that twinkle."

Tonks's wardrobe also developed after a long process. Her first look was what Tena describes as "weird eighties punk glamour night," with pointy high heel shoes, striped tights, and a pink tutu. Jany Temime felt that though the character was a bit more rebellious and light-hearted than others, she wanted her to appear strong. A pair of boots was swapped in, along with a long coat, hooded sweatshirt, fingerless gloves, and ripped tights, and Tena saw her character emerge. "The boots made her sturdy," Tena explains, "but they also trip her up. She's trying to act like an adult, but keeps screwing up and falling." A long red coat with military tailoring was worn for the climatic scenes at the Ministry between Death Eaters and the Order of the Phoenix. "She's ready for battle," says Tena, "but she still looks cool." Tonks's hair, pink in the books, was colored purple in order not to conflict with the pink associated with Dolores Umbridge. It turns red, in anger, and at the end of the battle scene, briefly white.

Tonks's flashy warrior togs are a direct contrast to the plain, drab clothes of her future husband, Remus Lupin. But as the Dark forces grow in *Harry Potter and the Half-Blood Prince*, Tonks becomes more serious. Her hair is now brown with a subtle purple rinse, and her clothes show more maturity. "Dark times, dark hair," Tena suggests. For *Harry Potter and the Half-Blood Prince*, Tena is seen in her own hair instead of the purple wig, and her outfits are created with softer textures and muted colors, although the palette stayed the same. "She's in love, and a bit more girly. But she does bring that adult aspect, she has to. She's still wearing those boots. There's just less twinkle." For *Harry Potter and the Deathly Hallows – Part 1* and *Part 2*, Jany Temime designed maternity clothes for Tonks for the Weasley wedding, dressing her in a floating silk fabric.

TONKS'S WAND

Nymphadora Tonks's wand is thin, with a striped shaft of two different woods. The handle resembles a Jack in the Pulpit flower, with a deep curve that allows for a strong grip on the end, which actress Natalia Tena only realized on the last film, *Harry Potter and the Deathly Hallows – Part 1*. "I thought I had worked out the right way to hold it," she admits. "And even had extensive wand training for *Order of the Phoenix*. But it wasn't until the wedding in *Part 1* that I realized that my wand had a little nook to work with!"

FIRST APPEARANCE:
Harry Potter and the Order of the Phoenix

ADDITIONAL APPEARANCES:
Harry Potter and the Half-Blood Prince
Harry Potter and the Deathly Hallows – Part 1
Harry Potter and the Deathly Hallows – Part 2

HOUSE:
Hufflepuff

OCCUPATION:
Auror

MEMBER OF:
Order of the Phoenix

ADDITIONAL SKILL SET:
Metamorphagus

INSET: *Natalia Tena as Nymphadora Tonks;* OPPOSITE: *Tena poses in her final outfit for Harry Potter and the Order of the Phoenix,* with the briefly seen white wig; LEFT TOP AND BOTTOM: *Costume concepts for Tonks's colorful outfits by Jany Temime, sketched by Mauricio Carneiro for* Order of the Phoenix; RIGHT: *A metamorphmagus, Tonks can transform her appearance at will, as seen in concept artwork by Rob Bliss for* Order of the Phoenix.

"Don't call me Nymphadora!"

Tonks, *Harry Potter and the Order of the Phoenix*

Kingsley Shacklebolt

Although it is Kingsley Shacklebolt who comments upon Albus Dumbledore's noticeable style, the Order of the Phoenix member is no slouch when it comes to flair. Actor George Harris was partially instrumental for the look of the character. "I came down to a fitting," recalls Harris, "and I was wearing an Agbada, which is a Nigerian ceremonial gown. Underneath that, I had on a pair of Kota trousers, like Indian pajamas." Jany Temime liked what she saw and decided that not everyone in the Ministry needed to wear a suit. She and Harris built upon the idea and assigned Shacklebolt an African heritage not specified in the books. The heavy Agbada robes he wears are embellished with beads, applique, and embroidery inspired by African motifs, with piping around the border. "I love to wear beads and bangles," he says, "so in addition to the earring that was indicated in the books, I wanted the beads, which make me feel very comfortable."

Shacklebolt's cap is also Nigerian-based. Having filmed in some very cold locations, the bald-headed actor knows that wearing a hat will help keep him warm. "But I also felt that the hat would, in a way, keep Shacklebolt's power from escaping. He has a quiet strength and wants to keep a lid on it." Literally. The hat is created from shot silk, which reflects light differently from different angles, and so shifts its color hues, in this case between blue, purple, and black.

FIRST APPEARANCE:
Harry Potter and the Order of the Phoenix

ADDITIONAL APPEARANCES:
Harry Potter and the Deathly Hallows – Part 1
Harry Potter and the Deathly Hallows – Part 2

OCCUPATION:
Auror, personal bodyguard to Muggle Prime Minister, Temporary Minister for Magic

MEMBER OF:
Order of the Phoenix

PATRONUS:
Lynx

SHACKLEBOLT'S WAND

Kingsley Shacklebolt's wand is a combination of several woods put together with a very organic structure in their design. Actor George Harris felt that though his character's costume is "flashy, he wouldn't have any big flashy wand moves. Economy is very, very important in the Order. His tendency is to be quite quick and very effective."

"You may not like him, Minister, but you can't deny Dumbledore's got style."

Kingsley Shacklebolt, *Harry Potter and the Order of the Phoenix*

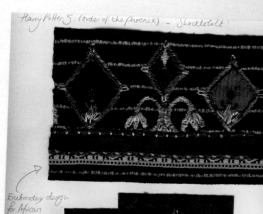

Harry Potter 5. (order of the phoenix) – Shacklebolt

Embroidery design for African Inspired hat

Embroidered buttons for jacket cuffs

African Inspired applique Motif, with hand embroidery – for Shirt front

INSET: *George Harris as Kingsley Shacklebolt;* OPPOSITE CENTER: *Jany Temime's sumptuous design for Shacklebolt's robes, sketched by Mauricio Carneiro for Harry Potter and the Order of the Phoenix;* OPPOSITE RIGHT: *Fabric samples showing the embroidery details;* TOP: *An early concept drawing of Shacklebolt by Rob Bliss;* ABOVE: *In Dumbledore's office with Auror John Dawlish (Richard Leaf), Dolores Umbridge, and Minister for Magic Cornelius Fudge (Robert Hardy);* RIGHT: *As with Dumbledore, you've got to admit that Shacklebolt has style.*

Chapter 7

DARK FORCES

LORD VOLDEMORT

FIRST APPEARANCE:
Harry Potter and the Sorcerer's Stone

ADDITIONAL APPEARANCES:
Harry Potter and the Chamber of Secrets
Harry Potter and the Goblet of Fire
Harry Potter and the Order of the Phoenix
Harry Potter and the Half-Blood Prince
Harry Potter and the Deathly Hallows – Part 1
Harry Potter and the Deathly Hallows – Part 2

HOUSE:
Slytherin

OCCUPATION:
Dark Lord

ADDITIONAL SKILL SET:
Parseltongue

Lord Voldemort had been seen in fleeting glimpses or flashbacks for the first few Harry Potter films. In *Harry Potter and the Sorcerer's Stone*, the noncorporeal He Who Must Not Be Named shares his body with Defense Against the Dark Arts Professor Quirrell. Actor Ian Hart's face and voice were refashioned digitally to create the Dark wizard. Voldemort's first corporeal appearance comes in *Harry Potter and the Goblet of Fire*, where he is "reborn" through a ritual performed by Peter Pettigrew, and much discussion took place as to what the fully realized Voldemort would look like. When Ralph Fiennes was cast in the role, he was shown concept art of the character. "They'd taken photographs of me and morphed them into this frightening, reptilian-looking creature," Fiennes remembers. "That's pretty much when I thought, 'Oh, this would be cool to do!'"

Early designs had Voldemort wearing robes similar to ones seen in a flashback in *Harry Potter and the Sorcerer's Stone*. "I was initially handed this great, thick, black, heavy thing that just didn't work at all," Fiennes says. So Jany Temime took her cue from the rebirth of the Dark Lord. "He is newborn," she explains. "He has just gotten back his skin, so I thought his robe should be a second skin to him, like a membrane. We needed something very tactile, and simple and floaty." Temime also felt that the actor shouldn't be encumbered. "He has such wonderful arms, such expression when he walks. That should be seen." Producer David Heyman felt the same way. "It was important that he wasn't weighed down and that it wasn't ornate. The Death Eaters may enjoy the jewels and finery, but not Voldemort. He's

PRECEDING PAGE: *A Death Eater as imagined for* Harry Potter and the Order of the Phoenix *by artist Rob Bliss;* INSET: *Ralph Fiennes as Lord Voldemort;* LEFT: *Voldemort's robes designed by Jany Temime for* Order of the Phoenix, *sketched by Mauricio Carneiro;* ABOVE: *In a controversial scene in* Order of the Phoenix, *Harry sees Voldemort in Muggle clothes at King's Cross Station;* OPPOSITE: *Voldemort flanked by a Death Eater and Severus Snape at Malfoy Manor in* Harry Potter and the Deathly Hallows – Part 1.

renounced all that." But as Voldemort gains more substance, he gains more layers of silk for his robes. "He is more *there*," says Temime. "So every time he gains new strength, more layers of silk were added." By the time Voldemort appears in *Harry Potter and the Order of the Phoenix*, in his battle against Dumbledore in the Ministry, Fiennes is dressed in more than one hundred and sixty-five feet (fifty meters) of silk.

A most important consideration was the reptilian facial features that Voldemort exhibits. "When we began designing Voldemort," recalls Nick Dudman, "we knew that we wanted him to be bald. Fortunately, Ralph Fiennes agreed to shave his head, because a bald cap is not only the most obvious effect, I think, it would have added two more hours in the makeup chair." Dudman and his conceptual artists felt that Voldemort's skin should have a translucent quality, showing all the veins. "We started with the idea of airbrushing them on, and we convinced one of the crew who was bald to be a test case for the technique. But this would have had the actor standing for up to six hours for the air brushing." Dudman credits key prosthetic makeup artist Mark Coulier with coming up with an idea that saved them all. "Mark suggested that we could create the same effect by copying the air-brushing design onto paper in sections and make them into transferable tattoos. These would line up and link together over his whole head. And we could add tiny dots on them that would line up with the registration points on Ralph's head, neck, and shoulders, so there would never be a problem with continuity. Brilliant." The transfers were produced on a clear material that has a slight sheen to it, which added to the "clammy, creepy, unhealthy" look of Voldemort's skin.

The filmmakers were very pleased with the look of the skin, but producer David Heyman was adamant about recreating Voldemort's snakelike, slit nose. They had already made a concession about not using contact lenses for Voldemort's red eyes. "We wanted to really feel and get into Ralph's eyes," says Heyman, "to really dig deep into Voldemort's. With red eyes, you're drawn more to the redness than you are by the lack of emotion behind them." Nick Dudman experimented on a life cast, chopping off the nose and sculpting a flattened face that was then cyber-scanned and digitally morphed to Fiennes's face. The effect worked to Heyman and the other filmmaker's satisfaction, but then the challenge was how to actually do it. "You could not do it with a prosthetic," avers Dudman. "It would look like a muzzle, and would take away part of the actor's face." It was obvious the effect had to be done digitally—and frame-by-frame. "But by doing this, he didn't have to act through a mask, which was the fear." Fiennes was grateful for the decision. "It's the sort of part where you are easily tempted to cover an actor," he says. "Prosthetics block the expression when you wear all that stuff. They put pieces on to cover my eyebrows, but I wear nothing around my mouth or neck, so the muscles of my face were not held back by too much stuff stuck onto them. I would prefer to do it just by the energy and through the acting of it, rather than through how it looks. Having said that, I would think everyone was very pleased." Having unrestricted movement was a boon to the actor, significantly when he first populates his new body. "We see him touching, feeling his head, feeling his face, feeling how a muscle might move, or what it's like to walk again—testing this whole new body for the first time." Voldemort's look was completed from head to toe. "It just didn't feel right that he would have shoes on," Fiennes continues. "He's just come out of this cauldron. So they gave me these feet with claws." Dudman also gave him false teeth, which lowered his gum line and "made his teeth just nasty," he says. "So you've got the character as described in the books, but it was still very much Ralph. Because, you know, I've always believed if you hire somebody like him, you don't make him invisible cause that's what you're paying for!"

In *Harry Potter and the Deathly Hallows – Part 2*, as the Horcruxes are destroyed, Voldemort's appearance subtly changes. "Voldemort's soul reduces as we watch," explains Dudman. "He becomes more hollow-eyed. His skin starts to crack and he develops little lesions. He literally breaks down."

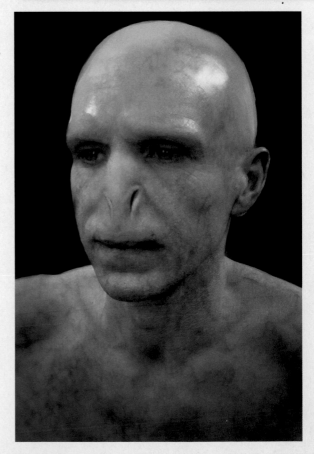

Eye Ideas 1 · HP4 PC 296b · Blood shot · grey/green

OPPOSITE: *Visual development artwork by Paul Catling entitled "Voldemort rising"*; TOP AND ABOVE: *Digital ideas for Voldemort's eyes and nose, also by Paul Catling, all for* Harry Potter and the Goblet of Fire.

VOLDEMORT'S WAND

W hat I had in mind for Lord Voldemort's wand," says concept designer Adam Brockbank, "was that it was probably carved from a human bone. So you've got this fine, tapering, sharp design. And you can see the honeycomb of the bone in the end section, which comes to the top of the bone, the joint, and then there's a hook on the end, like a claw. It's like a bony, evil finger." Actor Ralph Fiennes had a very distinctive way of holding the wand. "He never holds it like everyone else does," observes Pierre Bohanna. "It's always at the tips of his fingers. It's a very sensitive instrument, as far as he's concerned, so he's always holding it out, and it's always above his head, but it's always at the tips of his fingers."

TOP: *Voldemort surrounded by Death Eaters, by Paul Catling, for* Harry Potter and the Goblet of Fire; *OPPOSITE: Early visual development artwork of Lord Voldemort for* Harry Potter and the Sorcerer's Stone; *RIGHT: The fully corporeal Voldemort's first face-to-face confrontation with Harry Potter in* Goblet of Fire; *special effects have not yet removed his nose and altered Fiennes's skin; LEFT: Concept artwork of Voldemort's wand by Adam Brockbank.*

"Harry Potter, the boy who lived . . . come to die."

Voldemort, *Harry Potter and the Deathly Hallows – Part 2*

TOM MARVOLO RIDDLE

Voldemort is seen in his younger incarnation, Tom Marvolo Riddle, in several of the films. Christian Coulson played Tom as a teenager from fifty years earlier, in *Harry Potter and the Chamber of Secrets*, wearing school robes with a two-piece suit jacket underneath. The youngest version of Tom was seen in *Harry Potter and the Half-Blood Prince*, when he meets Dumbledore for the first time. Riddle is living at an orphanage, and so Jany Temime dressed actor Hero Fiennes-Tiffin (Ralph Fiennes's nephew) in a nineteenth-century institutional-style outfit of gray shorts, gray socks, gray shirt, and gray jacket. Frank Dillane took over the teenage Riddle in the same movie, as a student of Horace Slughorn. Dillane required the most makeup work of the three, needing blue contact lenses to match the color of Fiennes's eyes, pale pancake makeup to lighten his skin, and a brunette wig.

OPPOSITE: *A black-coated Voldemort envisioned by Paul Catling for* Harry Potter and the Goblet of Fire; THIS PAGE: *Tom Riddle's early years before and in Hogwarts were played by (left) Hero Tiffin-Fiennes at age 11, in a publicity photo for* Harry Potter and the Half-Blood Prince, *and (bottom left) Frank Dillane at age 16, in* Half-Blood Prince; BELOW: *Costume sketches by Mauricio Carneiro for* Half-Blood Prince.

shorts

shirt back

shirt front

coat back

PETER PETTIGREW

"Peter Pettigrew is a very shrewd, cowardly, weak, conniving, audacious, lying little character that is always ready to save his own skin. Apart from that, he's very nice and rather handsome," says Timothy Spall, who plays the human form of the rat known as "Wormtail" to the Marauders and "Scabbers" to the Weasley family. "This is a man who's been a rat for the last thirteen years," explains *Harry Potter and the Prisoner of Azkaban* director Alfonso Cuarón. "And so he still has to behave and look like a rat." Spall "went for it," continues Cuarón. "His ears were pointy, and had hair in them. Then I said, let's have a lot of hair coming out of your nose and let's add two big teeth in the front and have hair on your knuckles." The director found this all delightfully creepy. Of course, Spall was given long fake incisors and, "Since he uses his hands to express his character, we put on very nasty nails that were like little claws," says Amanda Knight. Along with Eithne Fennell, the hair and makeup artists also tried to invoke the various rats who played Scabbers, whether real or animatronic, in their vision for Pettigrew. "We tried to get the texture and the color of Wormtail's wig to match the Scabbers rat," explains Fennell. "We gave him bald patches and scaly skin."

"You are not born a rat," Jany Temime explains. "You have to *become* the rat. So what he wore needed to make him *feel* like a rat." Temime was able to work with the early seventies look of the Marauders for Pettigrew's clothing, allowing that the shape of that style was easily adaptable. Pettigrew's suit had a high collar that truncated his neck so it was barely visible, and the actor wore high-heeled Cuban boots that raised him up as if he was tip-toeing on paws, to give him the illusion of shortened lower legs. His striped jacket and pants combo are made of a fuzzy woolen fabric that was given a silvery sheen to mimic fur. Calculated rips and holes in the material give it a fringed effect and Temime made sure that a good clump of fringe was placed at the back so it almost appears as if he has a tail. Timothy Spall wore a green screen material on his "missing" finger for his first appearance in *Prisoner of Azkaban*; for *Harry Potter and the Goblet of Fire* and *Harry Potter and the Half-Blood Prince*, after he cuts off his right hand, the silver replacement was a combination of digital and practical effects.

FIRST APPEARANCE:
Harry Potter and the Prisoner of Azkaban

ADDITIONAL APPEARANCES:
Harry Potter and the Goblet of Fire
Harry Potter and the Order of the Phoenix
Harry Potter and the Half-Blood Prince
Harry Potter and the Deathly Hallows – Part 1

HOUSE:
Gryffindor

OCCUPATION:
Rat

MEMBER OF:
Order of the Phoenix, Death Eaters

ADDITIONAL SKILL SET:
Animagus ("Wormtail," a rat)

"Ron! Haven't I been a good friend? A good pet? You won't let them give me to the Dementors, will you? I was your rat . . ."

Peter Pettigrew, *Harry Potter and the Prisoner of Azkaban*

PETTIGREW'S WAND

Prop modeler Pierre Bohanna describes the design of Peter Pettigrew's wand as "Essentially a snake turning back on itself. Its head is on the handle, facing toward its tail, the tail being the tip of the wand." The original casting was carved from a piece of ebony wood. "The wand is supposed to be an extension of your character," says Adam Brockbank. "It must have been an interesting moment for the actors when they first picked up their wand."

INSET: *Timothy Spall as Peter Pettigrew;* OPPOSITE RIGHT: *Pettigrew in* Harry Potter and the Half-Blood Prince, *before special effects removes his missing (blue-screened) finger;* ABOVE LEFT AND OPPOSITE LEFT: *Pettigrew in various stages of transformation into Scabbers the rat, by Rob Bliss for* Harry Potter and the Prisoner of Azkaban; ABOVE CENTER: *Wormtail's suit for Prisoner of Azkaban, sketched by Laurent Guinci;* RIGHT: *Spall strikes a rodent-like pose in a publicity photo for* Half-Blood Prince.

Bellatrix Lestrange

It was imperative to actress Helena Bonham Carter that her character of Bellatrix Lestrange look sexy. "I've done witches before and I've done the hag look and I thought for this I want to be sexy." Bonham Carter reasoned that even though Bellatrix had been in Azkaban prison for fourteen years, "She had once been intensely glamorous but has sort of gone to seed." Bellatrix is seen briefly at first in *Harry Potter and the Order of the Phoenix* in a sack-like Azkaban prisoner uniform, but for her next appearance, Bonham Carter worked with Jany Temime to give Bellatrix a curvy shape. Bellatrix's dress, from a time before she went to prison, "may have once been beautiful," says Temime, "but now it's ragged and damaged. Of course, it had to be an old but chic rag." Threads hang down from its hem, laces are twisted, and the fit is a bit off. The waist of the dress, which is embroidered with silver spirals, is cinched in by a thin leather corset that is haphazardly stitched. The dress was so delicate that it couldn't be washed, so six copies needed to be made just for Helena Bonham Carter.

It is Bellatrix's hair and makeup that exemplify the true twisted nature of the Death Eater. Makeup artist Amanda Knight consulted with Bonham Carter about her look. "Helena wanted to have rotten teeth and nasty nails that were long and gnarled," she recalls. "I remember her painting bags underneath her eyes and sinking her cheeks to make herself look evil and nasty—but then counteracting that with lots of eye shadow, dark lipstick, and loads of mascara and eyeliner." Bellatrix's hair, a mixture of dreadlocks, curls, and way too much teasing is, as Bonham Carter describes it, "conspicuous." Bellatrix was also outfitted with several silver jewelry pieces that echo her gaunt, predatory air: she wears rings of a bird's skull and a bird's claw clutching her thumb, and a pendant with the same bird skull.

INSET: *Helena Bonham Carter as Bellatrix Lestrange;* OPPOSITE AND RIGHT: *Bellatrix's Azkaban prison photo and a wanted poster created by the graphic arts department seen in* Harry Potter and the Order of the Phoenix; LEFT AND ABOVE: *Costume sketch of Bellatrix's prison garb for* Order of the Phoenix *and a hooded coat for* Harry Potter and the Half-Blood Prince, *both sketched by Mauricio Carneiro.*

WANTED

BY THE MINISTRY OF MAGIC

BELLATRIX LESTRANGE

BELLATRIX LESTRANGE IS A KNOWN DEATH EATER. CONVICTED MURDERER. FUGITIVE FROM AZKABAN.

★ APPROACH WITH EXTREME CAUTION! ★

IF YOU HAVE ANY INFORMATION CONCERNING THIS PERSON, PLEASE CONTACT YOUR NEAREST AUROR OFFICE.

REWARD

THE MINISTRY OF MAGIC IS OFFERING A REWARD OF 1,000 GALLEONS FOR INFORMATION LEADING DIRECTLY TO THE ARREST OF BELLATRIX LESTRANGE

FIRST APPEARANCE:
Harry Potter and the Order of the Phoenix

ADDITIONAL APPEARANCES:
Harry Potter and the Half-Blood Prince
Harry Potter and the Deathly Hallows – Part 1
Harry Potter and the Deathly Hallows – Part 2

HOUSE:
Slytherin

OCCUPATION:
Death Eater

Bellatrix's first appearance in *Harry Potter and the Half-Blood Prince* is with her sister Narcissa as they arrive in a rainstorm at the family home of Severus Snape. Each sister wears a hooded coat, in their own inimitable way. "Narcissa has much more class," says Jany Temime, "and wears everything better. But for this, I wanted them both to look like little mice drowning in the rain." Beneath her long leather coat, Bellatrix wears a dress made of a rich velvety velour that is in much better condition than her previous attire. Her face is less sunken, and more appropriately madeup. "My teeth are much cleaner," says Bonham Carter, "although I really liked the awful version." Her lips and nails are painted red. "After that," says Temime, "Bellatrix goes to war. For this she wears a fuller corset, which to me was like armor." The corset is held together by toggles that, once again, resemble a bird skull. Bellatrix wears long protective sleeves that are laced to the shoulders of her full-torso corset, and her hair is piled atop her head. "She clearly has a personality disorder," laughs Bonham Carter, "because she always thinks she looks gorgeous."

BELLATRIX'S WAND

The handle of Bellatrix Lestrange's wand has a gentle curve, roughly inscribed with runic symbols. But then it quickly plummets into a shape that resembles the talon of a bird of prey. "I have the best wand," states Helena Bonham Carter. "It gives me a long arm and it's good for doing your hair." Bonham Carter had a slight mishap during the filming of the Ministry battle in *Harry Potter and the Order of the Phoenix* with Matthew Lewis (Neville Longbottom). "I thought I could brandish the wand sort of like a Q-tip and clean out his ear. Sort of torture it. But unfortunately he moved toward the wand and it actually perforated his eardrum." Fortunately, Lewis healed within a few days, affirming that, "Helena plays her character really well."

Hermione as Bellatrix

For *Harry Potter and the Deathly Hallows – Part 2*, Jany Temime undertook creating an outfit that would be worn by both Helena Bonham Carter and Emma Watson, when Hermione takes Polyjuice Potion in order to access the Lestrange's vault in Gringotts bank. Temime decided that the best approach was to fashion a coat with a short cape that would essentially hide the differences between the younger and older woman's silhouettes. Bonham Carter studied Watson's physical mannerisms as Hermione and was provided notes from the actress on how to play the part. The research was obviously effective—Jany Temime admits to being fooled when she saw Bonham Carter as "Hermione as Bellatrix" walking around the studio and thought it was Watson.

"My Lord, I'd like to volunteer myself for this task. I want to kill the boy."

Bellatrix Lestrange, *Harry Potter and the Deathly Hallows – Part 1*

OPPOSITE TOP: *Helena Bonham Carter holds Matthew Lewis hostage in front of a blue screen for* Harry Potter and the Order of the Phoenix; *OPPOSITE CENTER: A publicity photo for* Harry Potter and the Half-Blood Prince; *ABOVE: Costume reference of Bellatrix's coat worn in* Half-Blood Prince.

TOP: *Emma Watson is doused with water for a scene shot on a green-screen set after her character emerges from a lake;* ABOVE: *Ron, Harry, and the Polyjuice-potioned Hermione prepare to Apparate to Gringotts Bank, both in* Harry Potter and the Deathly Hallows – Part 2.

DEATH EATERS

FIRST APPEARANCE:
Harry Potter and the Goblet of Fire

ADDITIONAL APPEARANCES:
Harry Potter and the Order of the Phoenix
Harry Potter and the Half-Blood Prince
Harry Potter and the Deathly Hallows – Part 1
Harry Potter and the Deathly Hallows – Part 2

Death Eaters storm the grounds around the Quidditch World Cup in *Harry Potter and the Goblet of Fire*, signaling the return of Voldemort's Dark forces. "They were only seen in silhouette," says Jany Temime, "during the attack at the World Cup or in the fog at the graveyard, so I wanted a strong recognizable profile." Simple robes and pointed leather hoods created the shape, and plain skull masks covered their faces. When Voldemort's supporters, including Lucius Malfoy, appear in the Riddle family graveyard upon being summoned, these Death Eaters wear half masks that are digitally removed.

Temime initially envisioned the Death Eaters as "a secret society in evolution. And then, because the group becomes more and more official, they get almost a uniform for battle. You can imagine people meeting in secret and then changing their costume into something battle ready. The first time we see them, they are frightening. Then they become aggressive." Beginning in *Harry Potter and the Order of the Phoenix*, with forty Death Eaters, the capes were made from a much thicker material. Underneath, embroidered leather doublets were outfitted with a wand scabbard and protective arm cuffs and leg guards. For the battle waged in *Harry Potter and the Deathly Hallows – Part 2*, leather neck collars were added. The top of the hoods now draped over full-face masks, and fell into a serpentine trail down their backs. Costume fabricator Steve Kill was tasked with creating more than six

INSET: *Digital artwork portrays the special effects surrounding a Death Eater in* Harry Potter and the Goblet of Fire; *OPPOSITE: Costume reference of a Death Eater seen in* Goblet of Fire; *TOP: Death Eaters at the Quidditch World Cup;* RIGHT: *Death Eater costume design by Jany Temime for* Harry Potter and the Order of the Phoenix, *drawn by Mauricio Carneiro.*

ABOVE: *Director Mike Newell goes over the scene in Little Hangleton graveyard where the Death Eaters have assembled in* Harry Potter and the Goblet of Fire; BELOW AND OPPOSITE TOP RIGHT: *Jany Temime's simple silhouette for the Death Eaters in a costume illustration drawn by Mauricio Carneiro;* OPPOSITE LEFT: *Visual development artwork of Death Eater wands by Ben Dennett;* OPPOSITE RIGHT: *An elaborate Death Eater costume drawn by Paul Catling.*

hundred Death Eater outfits for *Harry Potter and the Deathly Hallows – Part 2*—two hundred for actors, and another four hundred for their doubles and stunt doubles. "We were given instructions by Jany Temime," says Kill, "that for the majority of the Death Eaters she wanted something simple because they were of a low grade. Then there are the aristocratic ones that surround Voldemort, so more ornate patterns were required." The most elaborate work went on the ten closest "lieutenants" of the Dark Lord, who each wore a unique design that indicated more their wealth than their rank. Female Death Eaters not only required smaller versions of the costumes, but the tracery and designs were less sophisticated as it was felt that anything more complicated would be overwhelming. Real leather was used, not only because it was actually less expensive than using a PVC-based material, but because "being the real thing, it looked like the real thing," says Kill. Metal workers added decorations and fastenings, and then hammered, sanded, and tarnished them to look battle worn.

Although the Death Eaters' faces were initially covered by half masks, concept artist Rob Bliss had always envisioned the masks to be full face. "The first time we see the Death Eaters, in *Goblet of Fire*, the masks are only partially on their faces," explains Bliss. "But in *Order of the Phoenix*, I thought it would be creepy to cover the whole face." Bliss felt that though there should be uniformity in the general silhouette, individuality could be expressed in the design of the masks, for personal identification and for prestige. "I think the Death Eaters have got quite showy aesthetics," says prop modeler Pierre Bohanna. "Their clothing is intricate, and so the idea of their masks being used to show-off isn't surprising." The masks almost evoke the torture devices of medieval times, and are decorated in early Celtic and runic symbols, and filigree similar to Mogul arabesque patterns of sixteenth and seventeenth century Islamic India. The masks are not painted but electroplated with silver. "This works on film so well," explains Bohanna. "It reacts well to light and it's got a quality that you just can't replicate with paint."

DEATH EATERS' WANDS

"We made an interchangeable selection of generic wands for the Death Eaters," says Draftsman Hattie Storey. "There were three basic types of handles and three types of sticks so that Pierre [Bohanna] could cast them in different colors and materials to make the huge number needed of different wands." Many of the hundreds of Death Eater wands sport skeletal designs or reinterpretations of the serpentine Dark Mark. The showier Death Eaters had, of course, showier wands. The scabbards created to hold the wands, based on seventeenth-century sword belts, had metalwork and designs that echoed their masks.

Chapter 8

MINISTRY OF MAGIC

MINISTRY PERSONNEL

Beginning with *Harry Potter and the Order of the Phoenix*, Jany Temime created suits and robes for the wizards and witches who work at the Ministry, choosing fabrics and styles that would seem "standard" for the employees and as ubiquitous as the Muggle three-piece suit. But with crowds of up to one hundred people, Temime also wanted diversity. She considered that the Ministry would host visitors from foreign lands, and whether from near or far, or towns or cities, these people would be of every social station, age, background, and ethnicity. "We tried to cover every single side of society," she iterates.

Temime did individualize the costumes for several specific Ministry characters. John Dawlish, an Auror and bodyguard to the Minister in *Harry Potter and the Order of the Phoenix*, wears a trench coat–like robe, with a capelet. Temime also designed generic Auror coats for *Harry Potter and the Half-Blood Prince* with many pockets, and a collar that can turn up to hide their face. Bartemius Crouch Sr., seen in both present day and past in *Harry Potter and the Goblet of Fire*, was dressed in a dark wizardy pinstriped suit topped by a Homberg hat. Rufus Scrimgeour, the new Minister for Magic in *Harry Potter and the Deathly Hallows – Part 1*, is also in

APPEARANCES:
Harry Potter and the Order of the Phoenix
Harry Potter and the Deathly Hallows – Part 1

APPEARANCES IN FLASHBACK:
Harry Potter and the Goblet of Fire
Harry Potter and the Half-Blood Prince

PRECEDING PAGE: *In* Harry Potter and the Order of the Phoenix, *Harry Potter and Arthur Weasley share a lift with other wizards, including (lower right) a goblin played by Warwick Davis;* LEFT AND OPPOSITE LEFT: *Jany Temime's designs for female and male Ministry personnel;* ABOVE AND OPPOSITE CENTER: *For* Order of the Phoenix, *Temime created costumes for generic Aurors and the lift operator;* OPPOSITE FAR RIGHT: *The designs became harder and darker in* Harry Potter and the Deathly Hallows – Part 1, *especially for the Ministry police force, all sketches by Mauricio Carneiro;* OPPOSITE TOP: *Arthur escorts Harry through morning rush hour at the Ministry.*

pinstripes, covered by a robe that resembles a Muggle Inverness cape. Temime considered that those who worked at the Ministry should not be too obvious in their wardrobe as they spent time in the Muggle parts of London and beyond. For *Harry Potter and the Order of the Phoenix*, she created dress robes for members of the Wizengamot, presided over by Minister Fudge. The robes are in either a black or a puce color known as "Victoria Lake," seemingly to imply rank, and the members wear hats that are reminiscent of ones worn by French and German judges.

As times get darker, Temime created a uniform for a police-type organization within the Ministry seen in *Harry Potter and the Deathly Hallows – Part 1*. "They had to be wizardy, of course, but I also wanted them to appear frightening, and impressive, and show a certain brutal strength." Temime dressed these elite enforcers in black, gray, and red, inspired by the security police units organized by the Axis powers in World War II. "It needed to be clearly identifiable as 'police' and yet still not have any reference to something you've seen before." In addition to their outfits, a specific type of wand this force would use was crafted. "It was decided that they would have something that looked tough on their belts," explains fabricator Steve Kill, "and have a handle like a police truncheon. And when they pull it out, it has a blade. It's very aggressive looking." Fifty of these special wands were created, which include a small sharpener implement. The wands sit in leather holsters that attach to belts for quick access.

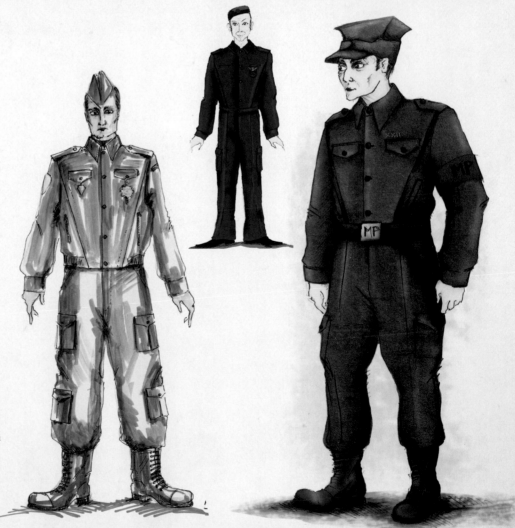

Cornelius Fudge

Actor Robert Hardy was elated when he was cast as the Minister for Magic, first seen in *Harry Potter and the Chamber of Secrets*, but disappointed during costume fittings when he wasn't shown the green suit and green bowler hat that his character wears in the books. "I was really fancying that green hat!" he says. The designers for *Harry Potter and the Chamber of Secrets* were just following director Chris Columbus's desire not to have too-strong colors in the costumes overtake the performances, and the Minister was dressed in earth tones—browns and mahoganies—in a Dickensian-style suit and robe. His hairstyle, with long sideburns, also fit in with the fashions of the Dickensian time period. For his appearance in *Harry Potter and the Prisoner of Azkaban* and for the rest of the series, Jany Temime rethought the Minister's garb, and followed her philosophy of dressing Ministry workers in less-than-obvious-but-still-wizard wear. Fudge now wears a dark pinstriped double-breasted coat that goes to his knees, and pinstriped dress robes, and finally got the bowler hat, albeit in black. His haircut is much shorter and straighter, losing the sideburns. Temime's attention to detail shows in the little touches that define a character; in *Harry Potter and the Prisoner of Azkaban*, Fudge wears that iconic sign of wealth, a fur hat, during his visit to Hogsmeade. After the battle in the Ministry at the climax of *Harry Potter and the Order of the Phoenix*, Fudge arrives at the Ministry late at night, apparently having thrown his coat and robes over a pair of buttoned-up striped pajamas. Hardy feels that the costumes exemplified "high politics" in an elegant way.

FIRST APPEARANCE:
Harry Potter and the Chamber of Secrets

ADDITIONAL APPEARANCES:
Harry Potter and the Prisoner of Azkaban
Harry Potter and the Goblet of Fire
Harry Potter and the Order of the Phoenix

OCCUPATION:
Minister for Magic

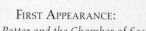

FUDGE'S WAND

Minister for Magic Cornelius Fudge's wand is used most notably to open the 422nd Quidditch World Cup final in *Harry Potter and the Goblet of Fire*. Using a *Sonorus* spell, his voice is broadcast through the stadium. Fudge's wand features two dimpled, white ball shapes, one at the end of the handle and the other at the transition to the shaft.

INSET: *Robert Hardy as Minister for Magic Cornelius Fudge;* OPPOSITE LEFT: *The Minister's style evolved over the course of the films. In* Harry Potter and the Chamber of Secrets, *his look was decidedly Dickensian;* OPPOSITE RIGHT: *Costume designs by Jany Temime of Fudge's bureaucratic wizard wear, sketches by Laurent Guinci;* TOP: *In the headmaster's office, Fudge watches Dumbledore disappear along with (left to right) Auror John Dawlish, Dolores Umbridge, and Kingsley Shacklebolt;* ABOVE: *The Minister for Magic is pressed for comments about Voldemort's return in* Harry Potter and the Order of the Phoenix.

RUFUS SCRIMGEOUR

People kept asking me 'Why are you not in the Harry Potter films?'" recalls actor Bill Nighy. "And I had no good answer to that." Nighy had previously worked with director David Yates several times and was filming a project with him when Yates was hired for *Harry Potter and the Order of the Phoenix*. "My heart leapt," he says. "I joked with him that now, perhaps, I would not be the only English actor who wasn't in Harry Potter. And yet," he adds sadly, "no one called." To his relief, Nighy was finally cast in the role of Rufus Scrimgeour, who succeeds Cornelius Fudge as the Minister for Magic in *Harry Potter and the Deathly Hallows – Part 1*.

Scrimgeour's outfit echoes the pin-striped bureaucratic feel as that of his predecessor. Jany Temime contrasted the thin, straight pinstripes with a scroll-patterned scarf and a wide, loose robe that resembles an Inverness cape. One cosmetic difference between the two Ministers is that Scrimgeour is described as having a leonine air and a mane of hair. "I loved that hair," says Nighy. "It reminded me of my youth, when I had that much hair."

Nighy and Yates discussed the role and its ramifications at length. "I thought of Scrimgeour as a kind of military figure," says Nighy, "but one who has been taken out of that world and placed into a less comfortable, public one. He's authoritative but his intentions are good. He may be stern but his heart is well disposed to Harry, Ron, and Hermione." Scrimgeour's first on-screen appearance harkens back to the rousing, assuring speeches given by Prime Minister Winston Churchill during World War II. "It's very Churchillian, in that Scrimgeour is saying that the state is strong enough to protect them, but I wanted to give it a bit of ambiguity. Perhaps he wasn't completely convinced, given the forces against which they are pitted." Nighy stood in front of more than one hundred actors when he delivered the speech. "And I felt like I was addressing the world, which made it very exciting. I hadn't expected that."

INSET AND OPPOSITE: *Bill Nighy as Minister for Magic Rufus Scrimgeour, who briefly held the office in* Harry Potter and the Deathly Hallows – Part 1; RIGHT: *Scrimgeour disperses Dumbledore's bequests to Hermione, Ron, and Harry prior to Bill and Fleur's wedding.*

FIRST APPEARANCE:
Harry Potter and the Deathly Hallows – Part 1

OCCUPATION:
Minister for Magic

"These are dark times, there is no denying."

Rufus Scrimgeour, *Harry Potter and the Deathly Hallows – Part 1*

Chapter 9

FAMILIES

VERNON, PETUNIA & DUDLEY DURSLEY

The one thing Vernon and Petunia Dursley, the Muggle aunt and uncle of Harry Potter, *do not* want to be is different. Judianna Makovsky agreed that they should not stand out, but in a world of wizards, the Dursleys should also not be a caricature. "I think the Dursleys were the most fun to dress," says Makovsky, "but we didn't want them to be a cartoon. People are scarier if they appear normal. We didn't want to beat the audience over the head with ugly outfits." Jany Temime, who took over costuming duties on *Harry Potter and the Prisoner of Azkaban*, agrees with Makovsky's approach. "They are bourgeois, lower middle class, which is nothing wrong, but it's very conventional. Being proper for them is being exactly like their neighbor. Being different is frightening for them."

Fiona Shaw has a great fondness for her character, Petunia, who is, according to her, "just a bit barking. I often play much grander historical characters in the theater. So it's actually wonderful to play the stress of the everyday housewife." Shaw participated in discussions with the costumers about her wardrobe. "I think we started off modestly. I started out with pearls and a cardigan, then cashmere and a tweed skirt, outfits that are about twenty years out of date. As the films progressed, I dress more outrageously, like my crazy daisy dress in *Harry Potter and the Order of the Phoenix*,

FIRST APPEARANCE:
Harry Potter and the Sorcerer's Stone

ADDITIONAL APPEARANCES:
Harry Potter and the Chamber of Secrets
Harry Potter and the Prisoner of Azkaban
Harry Potter and the Order of the Phoenix
Harry Potter and the Deathly Hallows – Part 1

OCCUPATIONS:
Businessman, housewife,
and Smeltings Academy student

PRECEDING PAGE: *A publicity photo of the Malfoys, father and son;* INSET: *Harry Melling as Dudley Dursley;* ABOVE: *Harry Potter with Uncle Vernon (Richard Griffiths) and Aunt Petunia (Fiona Shaw) in* Harry Potter and the Sorcerer's Stone; RIGHT: *Costume designs for Dursley summer wear by Jany Temime, including the daisy dress, sketch by Mauricio Carneiro;* OPPOSITE TOP: *Continuity shots taken for* Sorcerer's Stone; OPPOSITE BOTTOM: *The Dursleys in formal wear before a very important dinner in* Chamber of Secrets.

but it's still the same person. They're the stars of their world." Shaw did have a strange start to her costume when it needed to be adjusted for a specific scene. "There was a shot," she recalls, "where I had to look at an owl and an owl had to look at me. But the owls were very distracted by all the cameras. The owls thought the cameras were very interesting, much more interesting than me. So in the end, they hung dead mice from my apron so that the owls would absolutely look at me. Well, they were looking at the dangling mice. Never had to use dead mice before to get an actor to look at me!"

As Vernon Dudley, Richard Griffiths was dressed in simple suits that he feels reflected the changes in pater Dursley through the course of the films. Before the last film, *Harry Potter and the Deathly Hallows – Part 1,* Griffiths lost a bit of weight. "But that's all in keeping with the character, because I think as Vernon dwindles as a power he probably dwindles as a tubby, you know?" One of Griffiths's biggest challenges was during *Harry Potter and the Prisoner of Azkaban,* when he has to hang on as his sister Marge floats into the sky while her dog, Ripper, is clamped on to his ankle. "I was harnessed in a rig and tethered to Pam [Ferris] and the dog, whose name is George, was hanging on to me by his teeth. Thirty feet in the air, at least." A leather strap was wrapped around Griffiths's ankle for George to bite. "And the dog's growling and making noises—he's acting, I hope—and I'm trying to hold on, not sure if I'm more worried about the stunt or the dog!"

Harry Melling, who plays their spoiled son, Dudley, feels that the progression of his character was clearly shown in the costuming. "Looks-wise," explains Melling, "the first three films are fairly similar with my hair parted on the side and the kind of look that says, yes, Aunt Petunia has dressed me. In *Harry Potter and the Order of the Phoenix,* Dudley must be dressing himself, wearing high tops, and bike shorts, the vest and the red T-shirt. He's wearing chains around his neck and triple rings that go across one hand. And it gave me direction, it helped grow the character." For his final appearance, in *Harry Potter and the Deathly Hallows – Part 1,* the challenge of dressing Dudley was the opposite of "character growth," as Melling had lost more than sixty pounds before filming started. "When I read the script," recalls makeup effects designer Nick Dudman, "I thought, well, I won't have to worry about his character. Then I got a call from [producer] David Barron, who said 'You have to come and see this.' He turned up having lost half his body weight and was no longer this chubby, pugnacious kid." Dudman put Mark Coulier, his best "fat makeup" artist, on it, who created prosthetics for his chin, cheeks, and neck, and Melling wore a bodysuit with padding under his windbreaker.

OPPOSITE TOP LEFT: *The Dursleys—Dudley, Vernon, and Petunia—are surprised that Harry would receive any mail in* Harry Potter and the Sorcerer's Stone; OPPOSITE RIGHT: *Continuity shots of Richard Griffiths and Fiona Shaw for* Sorcerer's Stone; TOP: *Dudley despairs at being trapped in the snake tank at the London Zoo in* Sorcerer's Stone; ABOVE: *In a scene deleted from* Harry Potter and the Deathly Hallows – Part 1, *the cousins bid a final farewell.*

Aunt Marge Dursley

Marge Dursley walks into her brother's house, number 4, Privet Drive, in *Harry Potter and the Prisoner of Azkaban*. She leaves the house in a very different way, after Harry's anger with her thinly veiled insults about his parents cause him to lose control of his magic. "Well, she blows up like a balloon and floats away," says actress Pam Ferris, who plays Aunt Marge. "And it's a lot easier to say that than it is to do it, let me tell you! You need to eat an awful lot of baked beans and fizzy drinks to be able to lift off like she does," she teases. "I can tell you no more!"

But before Aunt Marge makes her "big mistake," the makeup department gave her her first unusual characteristic. As Marge is accompanied by her dog Ripper, "We all decided that she should have something like the dog," says Ferris. "Nothing too dramatic. We didn't want it to be like a 'Harry Potter' creature, just that she is a human who happens to look a bit like her dog." Ferris was fitted with a dental prosthetic that clipped onto her teeth to give her the under bite and sharp incisors of a bulldog, which she says she tried not to emphasize, but just "let them be there."

Aunt Marge's transformation was achieved with very little computer involvement. Director Alfonso Cuarón came to creature effects designer Nick Dudman and asked if the effect could be done practically. "And it was the one thing in the script I'd read that I thought would be digital!" says Dudman. Working with the makeup effects department, a plan was devised that would require four stages of makeup, but only needed two inflatable suits, pumped up by air tubes.

INSET: *Pam Ferris as Aunt Marge Dursley;* ABOVE: *Aunt Marge greets her nephew "Duddums," Dudley, in Harry Potter and the Prisoner of Azkaban;* RIGHT: *Vernon Dursley desperately tries to prevent his sister from floating away in artwork by Dermot Power;* OPPOSITE TOP: *Continuity shots of Marge's stunt double, Kelly Dent, at her most inflated;* OPPOSITE BOTTOM: *It's a lost cause as Marge lifts not only her brother, Vernon, but her dog, Ripper, as well.*

> *"Still here, are you?"*

Aunt Marge, *Harry Potter and*
the Prisoner of Azkaban

"There were inflatable gloves for her hands and separate inflatable legs," explains Dudman, "all set off by a computer-controlled pneumatic pressure device. The hands could inflate any given joint in any order." Pam Ferris spent up to five hours in the makeup chair having small prosthetic pieces and expandable rubber bladders applied to her face and neck before getting into an inflatable suit, which weighed fifty pounds. "At the later stages I was so spherical that I couldn't sit down; I could barely walk! At my biggest, I'm about four-foot-six across." Inside each suit was a flying harness suspended on two wire rigs. One would lift or flip her, the other rig spun her around. Ferris received high praise from the cast and crew for her patience and good nature. "It was like she was in a straightjacket," says producer David Heyman. "Then hung up by wires and suspended, and she never complained once. Not once."

Jany Temime was also impressed at how the stunt was achieved. "We thought this is never, never going to happen. We needed to make thirty-eight tweed suits for Aunt Marge. Her shape becomes crazier and crazier, and by the end, she's just a big tweed ball."

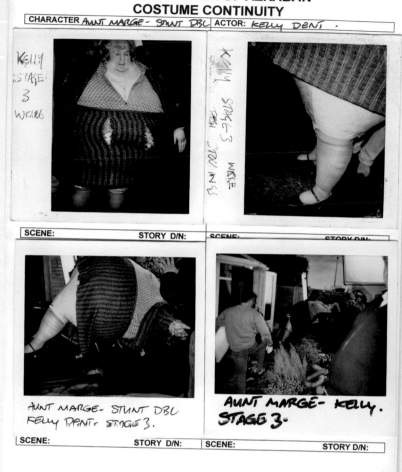

CHARACTER AUNT MARGE - STUNT DBL ACTOR: KELLY DENT.

AUNT MARGE - STUNT DBL KELLY DENT - STAGE 3.

AUNT MARGE - KELLY. STAGE 3.

XENOPHILIUS LOVEGOOD

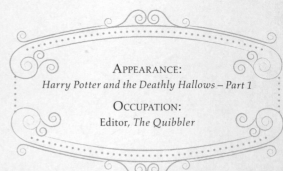

Xenophilius Lovegood, Luna Lovegood's father, works out of his house in the countryside as editor of *The Quibbler*. "This man has causes," says Jany Temime. "He believes in things. And because he lives in such an isolated world, I thought, he must work in his pajamas. You know, when you work at home, why should you dress?" When Harry, Ron, and Hermione visit Lovegood at his home, he wears a long striped shirt covered by a vest and a bathrobe-type coat that has seen better days. "I found that engine coat, that beautiful handwoven antique coat, which was a very natural organic thing." The coat and its two duplicates were "broken down," but instead of pulling threads out, "We added threads," says Temime. "We wanted there to be threads hanging from the hem and there just weren't enough.

"When I was fitting it to Rhys," Temime continues, "I wanted more layers to show the different layers of his personality." Ifans and Temime had worked together previously and began discussing this idea. "Something we thought of were the little patches," says Ifans, "which I suggested Luna has made for Xenophilius. I wanted some attachment to her because she's very present in the scene even though she's not actually there. So perhaps these would be things that she embroidered over the years for my birthday or her mother's birthday." "I remembered that Luna was always adorned in handmade jewelry," Temime adds. "So I had the idea that we could make a pieced waistcoat and each one of the pieces was something that Luna had stitched or appliqued for him. Then he would be wearing his daughter's work on his chest, because Luna is his world." The natural imagery that Luna displays in her own outfits and jewelry is well represented on the waistcoat, which is covered in butterflies and flowers, mythological creatures, Dirigible Plums, and images that resemble Luna's Gryffindor lion hat and the Durmstrang ship.

As Xenophilius, Rhys wears a long blond wig that echoes Luna's long tresses. "He's described in the book as having long golden hair," Ifans says. "He's also got a cross-eye in the book, which I can't really hold for very long. I did try a contact lens, but it was too excruciating. And I think it would have made him too comedic, in a way." While Ifans felt the character shouldn't be too funny, it didn't stop the actor from cracking up other actors on the set, something that's called "corpsing." Emma Watson, who was particularly adept at keeping a straight face, found him hysterical. "I just couldn't keep it together," she admits. "I couldn't stop laughing." Ifans nicknamed her "Giggles" by the end of their days filming together.

INSET: *Rhys Ifans as Xenophilius Lovegood;* LEFT: *Ifans poses for a costume reference shot of his "work" clothing for* Harry Potter and the Deathly Hallows – Part 1; OPPOSITE LEFT: *Details of the embroidered patches on Lovegood's waistcoat;* OPPOSITE BOTTOM RIGHT: *Costume design of the coat, sketch by Mauricio Carneiro;* OPPOSITE TOP RIGHT: The Quibbler *editor poses in his Weasley wedding clothes.*

APPEARANCE:
Harry Potter and the Deathly Hallows – Part 1

OCCUPATION:
Editor, *The Quibbler*

"What is it? Well, it's the sign of the Deathly Hallows, of course."

Xenophilius Lovegood, *Harry Potter and the Deathly Hallows – Part 1*

XENOPHILIUS'S WAND

Xenophilius Lovegood's wand "captured his eccentricities," says prop modeler Pierre Bohanna. "It's like a unicorn's horn with a beautiful, beautiful twist." Runic symbols are shallowly carved at the handle of the light-colored wood.

LUCIUS & NARCISSA MALFOY

When Jason Isaacs arrived at Leavesden Studios for costume and makeup consultations for his part of Lucius Malfoy in *Harry Potter and the Chamber of Secrets*, he was surprised that initial sketches for the character showed a man in a pin-stripe suit with short, dark hair. "I panicked slightly," Isaacs recalls, "because it looked just like me!" Isaacs didn't see a physical connection to Tom Felton's character and spoke with director Chris Columbus, who had already approved the sketches. "I thought, as Lucius despises Muggles, he wouldn't want to dress like one. I thought he'd wear outfits made of velvet and fur, and ornament himself in things that had been in his family for hundreds of years." Isaacs asked the costume department to help him show Columbus his ideas, including a provisional white-blonde wig, and the director was slowly persuaded to make the change. "'Is there anything else?' he asked me, and I said yes, I wanted a walking cane. And he said, 'Why, is there something wrong with your leg?'" Isaacs explained that he thought it would be an interesting affectation, and that his wand could come out of the cane, unlike other wizard's, who kept their wands in pockets. "Fortunately, Daniel Radcliffe was there and said that sounded cool. And more fortunately, Chris Columbus is a very open-minded, collaborative sort of man and let the original concept go."

Associate costume designer Michael O'Connor agreed that Lucius should suggest an establishment-type figure, "like bankers, people with a lot of money, and people with a very, very long bloodline or pedigree. He's from the old school of wizards and doesn't like those that aren't pure-bloods. So we started with that." The elder Malfoy's tailoring is sleek and slightly Edwardian, with high-necked long frock coats under an ermine-collared cape that is held together by one of several pieces of serpentine-style silver jewelry. For *Harry Potter and the Order of the Phoenix*, Jany Temime designed a quilted leather armor that Lucius—and other Death Eaters—wear under their hooded robes; Isaacs asserts this makes him feel like "a wizard ninja." And even though he still sports the cane, Lucius was given a wand holster that incorporates snake heads in its design for battle scenes. For *Harry Potter and the Deathly Hallows – Part 1* and *Part 2*, after Lucius returns from a stint in Azkaban, his costumes were distressed and his hair is disheveled as he had been beaten down from his experience.

Isaacs says he found Lucius easy to play and gives much credit to the costume and makeup departments. "I have these long, flowing robes, but with no pockets to stick my hands into, so I can't slouch. The cane also encourages me to stand in a particular way. And in order to keep my lovely, long blonde hair straight, I have to tilt my head back. It means I'm always looking down my nose at someone." Another credit he offers is to his inspiration for the development of Lucius's voice. "It drips with entitlement and superiority, like a snotty art critic. It's unctuousness with a very pinched, strangled sound." And the inspiration? "Well, when you're in the same film as Alan Rickman, who has set the bar very high for playing 'sinister,' you have to do something extreme!"

INSET: *Jason Isaacs as Lucius Malfoy;* OPPOSITE: *Isaacs demonstrates a perfect Lucius Malfoy sneer in a publicity photo for* Harry Potter and the Order of the Phoenix; RIGHT: *Sketches for Lucius's Death Eater robes for* Harry Potter and the Deathly Hallows – Part 2 *by Mauricio Carneiro.*

LUCIUS MALFOY

FIRST APPEARANCE:
Harry Potter and the Chamber of Secrets

ADDITIONAL APPEARANCES:
Harry Potter and the Goblet of Fire
Harry Potter and the Order of the Phoenix
Harry Potter and the Deathly Hallows – Part 1
Harry Potter and the Deathly Hallows – Part 2

HOUSE:
Slytherin

MEMBER OF:
Death Eaters

*"Is he alive? Draco.
Is he alive?"*

Narcissa Malfoy, *Harry Potter and
the Deathly Hallows – Part 2*

Actress Helen McCrory concedes that her character's name gave her insight into her look. "I mean, you just can't arrive looking like a mess when you're called Narcissa!" McCrory and Jany Temime looked at very European "aristocratic" cuts and lines and landed on a style that reflects the tailored couture of the 1950s. "Even though she's in a low period of her life," explains Temime, "she is still extremely elegant and chic." Narcissa's clothes reflect her own pure-blood status, her Slytherin heritage, and her devotion to her family. "The outfits are very tailored," says McCrory, "and have a lot of detail so that you feel these are clothes that her family has had for a while." The hooded and flared coat she wears at the beginning of *Harry Potter and the Half-Blood Prince* is an olive green, shot through with undulating silver lines almost scale-like in design. Temime wanted the clothes to have a very structured look, with "built-up shapes," and even inserted a wood frame into the shoulders of the coat. Later, on a visit with Draco to Borgin & Burkes, Narcissa wears a gray suit with an A-line skirt and a peplum-waisted short coat that sports cape-like sleeves and back. "Her clothes should have some mystery, and some strangeness," she says. "But are based in reality. At least, her reality."

For *Harry Potter and the Deathly Hallows – Part 1* and *Part 2*, Narcissa is hosting Voldemort and his followers in her house. "She is very much the lady of the manor," says Temime. For "receiving," as Temime calls it, she fabricated a black velour robe with a beige sheath dress underneath it. The robe has cuffs, pockets, and its front embellished with iridescent beads set in a winding, sinewy design. During the daytime meetings of the Death Eaters, Narcissa wears another short suit with a paneled front and cinched waist in a decidedly scaly fabric. Her long black robe is cloned for outdoor use in a thicker fabric with mink around its neck, silver bindings, and leather enhancements that, as always, curl around her cuffs and neckline.

Narcissa's hair is what Helen McCrory describes as "quite otherly. Helena [Bonham Carter] had filmed Bellatrix with dark hair, and they *are* sisters, so . . ." McCrory is a natural brunette, but the idea was suggested by hair designer Lisa Tomblin that as Narcissa had been with the Malfoys for so long, her hair would reflect both wizarding families. "We tried different types of blonde hair, and different configurations, and finally, we came up with this," Tomblin says, referring to Narcissa's mashup of blonde and brunette tresses. But McCrory feels that the hairstyle is a match to Narcissa's elegant style, and would be "recognizably chic in this world of witches and wizards."

NARCISSA MALFOY

FIRST APPEARANCE:
Harry Potter and the Half-Blood Prince

ADDITIONAL APPEARANCES:
Harry Potter and the Deathly Hallows – Part 1
Harry Potter and the Deathly Hallows – Part 2

HOUSE:
Slytherin

OCCUPATION:
Mother

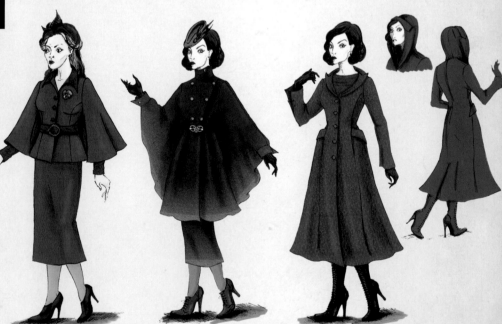

OPPOSITE LEFT: *Narcissa Malfoy (Helen McCrory) in her "wood-framed" coat for* Harry Potter and the Half-Blood Prince; OPPOSITE RIGHT: *Costume illustrations for Narcissa's wardrobe, drawn by Mauricio Carneiro;* TOP: *Narcissa draws her wand;* ABOVE: *Lucius Malfoy and his snake-tipped cane,* Harry Potter and the Goblet of Fire; RIGHT: *Concept art of Narcissa Malfoy's wand by Adam Brockbank.*

LUCIUS'S & NARCISSA'S WANDS

Lucius Malfoy's wand proudly proclaims his Slytherin roots, with its sleek black shaft topped by an open-mouthed silver snake's head with inset emerald eyes, which he encases in a walking stick. The snake head has replaceable teeth, as these would often break off when Isaacs used the cane too boisterously. For *Order of the Phoenix*, actor Jason Isaacs used a "public-school fencing style," he says. "I think watching the contrast of this formal style with Sirius Black's Azkaban-informed style is one of the enjoyable aspects of our wand battle. Not experts dueling with each other, but old adversaries."

Narcissa Malfoy's wand echoes the design of her husband's. "I tried to do a feminine version of Lucius's wand," says designer Adam Brockbank, "and then embedded silver studs into the black wood of her wand." Prop modeler Pierre Bohanna feels that the wands effectively represented their wizards. "It's all presentation with the Malfoys, I think. It's all to do with how you look rather than what the purpose is." Both Narcissa and Lucius use different, simple wands in *Deathly Hallows – Part 2*, as Lucius's wand is taken by Voldemort, and Narcissa gives her wand to her son, Draco.

Molly & Arthur Weasley

Just as a set designer will consider architectural shapes when creating a set, a costume designer muses on the silhouette of a character. Molly Weasley's silhouette is soft and motherly, "nicely rounded" as actress Julie Walters describes it. But "I was heartbroken on the first film," she states, "when Daniel Radcliffe thought that was all me." The silhouette was initially created not by cotton stuffing or fluffy wadding but by . . . bird seed. "I was admittedly worried while on the King's Cross Station set, with the pigeons and the owls." Her concern was well founded, and soon the silhouette was created in a more traditional way. Judianna Makovsky knew that Molly Weasley's silhouette would be covered in "crafty" clothing, as the Weasley's were not as well-off as other wizarding families and would have to "make do," though Molly's first appearance in *Harry Potter and the Sorcerer's Stone* is in her version of Muggle clothing, as she is at King's Cross Station.

The Weasleys' wardrobe was among *Harry Potter and the Chamber of Secrets* costume designer Lindy Hemming's favorites. Hemming consulted with production designer Stuart Craig about the look of The Burrow and took her cues from the country-wizard feeling of their home environment. "We knew from the books that Molly Weasley loved knitting, and decided that their house was probably a bit chilly now and again, and she didn't like ironing, so all their clothes became imbued with a woolly feeling. We went on a woolen tweed adventure!" The wool that was used to create the sweaters and scarves and crochet edging on other clothing items was purchased from vintage wool merchants. Tweeds and corduroys added additional textures and patterns, covered by kitschy aprons, all in the ginger-haired Weasleys' palette of earth tones in greens, oranges, and browns. Molly Weasley's costumes took roughly twelve weeks from start to finish, fitted around the padding Julie Walters wore.

INSET: *Mark Williams as the Weasley patriarch, Arthur;* TOP: *Molly Weasley in one of her homemade creations in* Harry Potter and the Chamber of Secrets; RIGHT: *Molly's coat for* Harry Potter and the Deathly Hallows – Part 2, *sketched by Mauricio Carneiro;* OPPOSITE: *The actors' warm relationship is evident in a publicity photo of Julie Walters and Mark Williams for* Harry Potter and the Order of the Phoenix.

TOP, ABOVE LEFT AND CENTER: *Costume concepts for Molly Weasley for* Harry Potter and the Half-Blood Prince *and* Harry Potter and the Order of the Phoenix *are seen in fully realized forms and in costume reference shots;* ABOVE RIGHT: *Casual home wear for Arthur Weasley for* Half-Blood Prince *seen in a costume reference shot;* OPPOSITE LEFT: *Sketch by Mauricio Carneiro;* OPPOSITE TOP: *Harry and the Weasleys en route to the Quidditch World Cup in* Harry Potter and the Goblet of Fire.

ARTHUR WEASLEY

FIRST APPEARANCE:
Harry Potter and the Chamber of Secrets

ADDITIONAL APPEARANCES:
Harry Potter and the Prisoner of Azkaban
Harry Potter and the Goblet of Fire
Harry Potter and the Order of the Phoenix
Harry Potter and the Half-Blood Prince
Harry Potter and the Deathly Hallows – Part 1
Harry Potter and the Deathly Hallows – Part 2

HOUSE:
Gryffindor

OCCUPATION:
Misuse of Muggle Artifacts Office,
Ministry of Magic

MEMBER OF:
Order of the Phoenix

"Tell me, what exactly is the function of a rubber duck?"

Arthur Weasley, *Harry Potter and the Chamber of Secrets*

Throughout the course of the Harry Potter films, Molly Weasley is "mother first and witch second," says Walters, except in the final battle for Hogwarts in *Harry Potter and the Deathly Hallows – Part 2.* "Normally she is the mother, but for this she is a fighter, and should look so," says Temime. "I was inspired by Spaghetti Westerns again."

Arthur Weasley's clothing took less time to construct. "We tried lots of suits with different old-fashioned shapes, borrowed from a costume house," explains Hemming, "to see how the silhouette would work on him to get an interesting body shape." Coordinating her decisions with associate costume designer Michael O'Connor, the head of the Weasley clan is dressed in a suit based on research into 1950s civil servants, and a wizardy pointed hat was added that would evoke the businessman's Trilby hat of that era. Mr. Weasley's robe is green, which O'Connor felt "would have been like a warehouse or uniform coat that he might have put on at work."

When Jany Temime took over costuming duties on *Harry Potter and the Prisoner of Azkaban*, she continued the Weasley tradition of reusing and renewing. "I think [Molly] recycles everything; she has to because there isn't a lot of money. Many things are second-hand." But Temime considered that Mrs. Weasley has "an amazing imagination. This old bedspread? She will make a coat of it. That dress might have been curtains." For many pieces for the Weasley family, clothing was purchased at contemporary shops and then distressed, altered, and redesigned with different buttons, old lace, and rickrack, and inevitably finished off with something knitted.

MOLLY'S & ARTHUR'S WANDS

Molly Weasley's wand is simple, but as Julie Walters affirms, "I felt like a warrior with it. It was heaven when I first got to use the wand." Walters worked with Paul Harris, the wand choreographer for *Harry Potter and the Deathly Hallows – Part 2,* and found that wielding a wand was quite different from other forms of fighting with arms. "There's nothing to actually hit, so you have a tendency to whack your arm around, which could get painful at the end of the day. Worth it, though. I absolutely loved my battle with Bellatrix."

Arthur Weasley's wand has what prop modeler Pierre Bohanna describes as "a sugar barley twist." The handle of the wand is finely turned, with a Jacobean feel to it. Actor Mark Williams felt his wand was very elegant. "I was quite fond of it," he recalls, "except that I developed a strange posture with it." The right-handed Williams found that he would consistently use his left hand to pick up the wand. "So my choreography became a bit twisted. Well, you can't say I didn't have my own personal style!"

In an epilogue that caps the Harry Potter film series in *Harry Potter and the Deathly Hallows – Part 2*, Harry and Ginny, and Ron and Hermione, bring their children to King's Cross station to send them off to Hogwarts School of Witchcraft and Wizardry on the Hogwarts Express. Jany Temime believes that "People's choices in styles don't really change that much through time." She kept to her palette of pinks and oranges, and blues and brown, and dressed them with the simple idea that though their careers might influence their fashion, this was a public but family-oriented occasion.

Harry Potter wears a dark blue jacket and trousers and a gray-blue shirt. "It's a designer jacket," she explains, "but understated. He doesn't need to show that he has money and power. He is Harry Potter." Temime put his wife, Ginny, in a soft blouse and skirt. "I thought this made a good balance in the couple. Ginny has always had a silent strength, but is always feminine." Hermione Weasley, née Granger, was dressed in a sharp shirt and blazer, but "still in jeans. I wanted to give her a square shoulder but still have it feel casual. Husband Ron," according to Temime, "wears something soft and brown and comfortable." Draco Malfoy appears in an elegant three-piece blue suit. Temime gave him Lucius Malfoy's ring and tie pin, to show that he had "taken over" his father's role. She thought that Draco would marry a trophy wife, but, "Wives always look like your mom. So I thought about his mom and I dressed her like that."

The question was then posed how to age the actors nineteen years, whether it should be done digitally or practically, and practical won out. However, when Daniel Radcliffe was tested wearing "thirty-eight-year-old makeup," standing next to an actual thirty-eight year old, it didn't quite work. "The experiences you have had shape you and change you, and that needed to be brought into the performance," says director David Yates. "And every thirty-eight year old looks different, because some people have naturally youthful looks and some people just age more quickly. Obviously, the danger is to go too far." The makeup was rethought and scenes were reshot.

Bonnie Wright was nine years old the first time she set foot on platform nine and three-quarters as Ginny Weasley. Ten years later, she offered a comment on shooting the end of the last Harry Potter film and the end of the entire Harry Potter film series. "The real ending for all of us is a difficult eventuality, even though it's imminent. But even though we are going to finish, anything that you do within film, or literature, or art—it's lasting. It's going to last forever. All the experiences I've had, and the people that I've been with—they're lovely

memories that have literally been captured on film. It's just going to be the best album that I could ever have to look back through."

OPPOSITE LEFT TO RIGHT: *The next generation of wizards assembles at King's Cross Station— Hugo Weasley (Ryan Turner, in front), Ron Weasley, Ginny Weasley Potter, Lily Luna Potter (Daphne de Beistegui), Harry Potter, Albus Severus Potter (Arthur Bowen), Hermione Weasley (née Granger), and Rose Weasley (Helena Barlow);* LEFT: *Draco Malfoy; son, Scorpius (Bertie Gilbert); and wife, Astoria (Jade Gordon);* FOLLOWING PAGE: *Costume designs by Jany Temime for Ariana Dumbledore and Aberforth Dumbledore for Harry Potter and the Deathly Hallows – Part 2, sketches by Mauricio Carneiro.*

First published in the United Kingdom and Australia in
2015 by:
TITAN BOOKS
A division of Titan Publishing Group Ltd
144 Southwark Street
London SE1 0UP
www.titanbooks.com

A CIP catalogue record for this title is available from
the British Library.

ISBN: 9781783296033

TITAN BOOKS

A division of Titan Publishing Group Ltd
144 Southwark Street
London SE1 0UP
www.titanbooks.com

Published by arrangement with Insight Editions,
PO Box 3088, San Rafael, CA 94912, USA.
www.insighteditions.com

Produced by

INSIGHT
EDITIONS

PO Box 3088
San Rafael, CA 94912
www.insighteditions.com

Publisher: Raoul Goff
Executive Editor: Vanessa Lopez
Production Editor: Rachel Anderson
Editorial Assistant: Greg Solano
Art Director: Jon Glick & Chrissy Kwasnik
Designer: Jenelle Wagner
Production Manager: Anna Wan and Lina sp Temena

Insight Editions would like to thank Victoria Selover,
Elaine Piechowski, Melanie Swartz, Kevin Morris, Ashley
Bol, George Valdiviez, Jamie Gary, Kat Maher, and Claire
Houghton-Price for their help and support throughout this
series, including *Harry Potter: The Creature Vault* and
Harry Potter: Magical Places from the Films.

ROOTS of PEACE   REPLANTED PAPER

Insight Editions, in association with Roots of Peace, will plant two trees for
each tree used in the manufacturing of this book. Roots of Peace is an
internationally renowned humanitarian organization dedicated to
eradicating land mines worldwide and converting war-torn lands into
productive farms and wildlife habitats. Roots of Peace will plant two
million fruit and nut trees in Afghanistan and provide farmers there
with the skills and support necessary for sustainable land use.

Manufactured in China by Insight Editions

10 9 8 7 6 5 4 3 2 1